"When it comes to a home, more than any other room, the kitchen can tell a story about the family that lives there. It's not just a place to prepare the family meal—it can tell you about their shared values and their comforts. It's a place to find refuge and a storehouse of memories."

—Bob Zuber, AIA, partner,
Morgante Wilson Architects (Evanston, Illinois)

In Detail Interiors added a personalized look to this kitchen using custom floating shelves with a gray-wash finish and a reverse arrow accent tile backsplash.

Barbara Ballinger ◆ **Margaret Crane**

Kitchen Conversations

SHARING SECRETS TO KITCHEN DESIGN SUCCESS

images
Publishing

A cozy nook in this elegant kitchen, by Ashley Sharpe in collaboration with Bilotta Kitchen & Home, includes a built-in desk. Kitchen desks, or work nooks, are making a comeback, often tucked away in a corner or non-traffic zone for privacy.

Contents

Foreword

Dr Jessica Lautz

Deputy Chief Economist and Vice President of Research at
The National Association of REALTORS®, Washington, DC

The Covid-19 pandemic changed how everyone lives and functions in their homes, worldwide. We have all adapted to a new way of living since then, but there remains one constant—home is the refuge. And the heart of that refuge is the kitchen.

Many people have moved since the start of the pandemic, fueled by the ability to work remotely or the desire to be closer to friends and family. Others invested in their current home by undertaking remodeling projects. Unsurprisingly, one of the most popular projects has been remodeling the kitchen.

A US study, *The 2022 Remodeling Impact Report*, by the National Association of REALTORS® (NAR) and The National Association of the Remodeling Industry (NARI), collated results on kitchen remodels. While most homeowners (87 percent) insist they would have remodeled their kitchen regardless of the pandemic, 25 percent of REALTORS® report an increased demand by homebuyers for a complete kitchen remodel since the beginning of Covid-19 in 2020.

When homeowners remodel, it is to add features and improve livability (25 percent) and to upgrade worn-out surfaces, finishes, and materials (25 percent). After remodeling, 94 percent of owners have a greater desire to spend more time at home. Eighty-six percent have increased enjoyment there and 85 percent feel a major sense of accomplishment when they think of their completed project. When ranked on a one to 10 Joy Score scale—a way to track enjoyment of your mind, body, and life on a daily basis—those who took on a complete kitchen remodel reported a score of 9.8. Forty-three percent of homeowners report the most important outcomes of remodeling are better functionality and increased livability.

The cost to take on a kitchen remodel can vary widely based on the materials chosen, the size of the kitchen, and any unforeseen complications. Based on the report, professional remodelers estimate a kitchen remodel for a typical home may cost $80,000, while REALTORS® report the estimated cost recovered is closer to $60,000. If homeowners were to sell, they could receive up to 75 percent return on the value of the recovered project, depending on the market.

While the study speaks to the data, *Kitchen Conversations* explores inspiring ideas, blueprints, photos, and personal narratives of homeowners and design professionals across the country [the United States], well beyond the data. Authors Barbara Ballinger and Margaret Crane aptly point out overlooked aspects of a kitchen remodel, such as functional electric outlets outfitted for countertop appliances and USB ports for the ever-present cell phone or iPad for recipes. The authors invite readers to consider the personality of lighting given all the possibilities with LEDs, the dos and don'ts of color, and how backsplash and flooring can change the dynamic of a room. And they also bring up kitchens of the future and all the changes in technology, sustainability, and equipment that have started to emerge.

The authors also understand the changing dynamic of family and home life. The kitchen is often in a multigenerational space where grandparents need to open cabinet doors and young children need places to perch for cookie making. And the room's increased importance has led to auxiliary spaces—from back pantries, laundries, and mud rooms to at-home bars, work nooks, pet spas, and more.

The pandemic has changed how we live within our home, but also outside the home. *Kitchen Conversations* understands that the kitchen is no longer confined to a room indoors; it has also expanded to the outdoors. Back yards have become family living spaces, a safe gathering spot for parties, and a sanctuary during the week to enjoy a brick-oven pizza and glass of wine.

Whether you are in the dream planning stages of the perfect kitchen, buying materials, and talking to a contractor or designer, or ready to embark on a DIY project, this book will motivate you and fuel excitement for the journey and the results.

I embarked on my own pandemic kitchen remodel, and I reflected on the process while reading this book. Planning with professionals who will guide the voyage and help keep it within your budget is worth the effort. The journey can be messy—even painful, at times—but the result is massively rewarding. Similar to the majority of homeowners in the report, my Joy Score is a solid 9.8, and I absolutely love to cook and entertain in my new eat-in kitchen. I was able to create a natural gathering space that provides warmth to family and guests alike. I know that after you read this book, you will be educated and enthused to tackle your own kitchen remodel.

Studio Pressman in Raleigh, North Carolina, and Los Angeles, California, run by architectural designer Yonatan Pressman, transformed a Silverlake, California, mission-style bungalow by placing the kitchen at its core. Red oak floors in a chevron pattern add sophistication, and an oak countertop provides a comfortable table ambiance.

Introduction

Barbara Ballinger & Margaret Crane

Imagine yourself at breakfast sitting at your serpentine-shaped island, reading the newspaper digitally and telling your smart faucet to give you a cup of water to make your oatmeal. You're studying a food blog on a screen that is superimposed on your backsplash. In your futuristic kitchen, you may even have a robot buddy to help you plan a healthy menu—your doctor has recommended you eat more veggies—and share the workload. "You've had too much meat and dairy this week. It's time for a vegetarian stew," the robot may say. If you've handled all the programming properly, your robot may even cook for you and announce, "Dinner's ready" and later clean up. Life will be a breeze.

The best kitchens dazzle, work hard, clean up well, last a decade or longer, provide a haven, and fulfill other dreams. But they don't appear magically with a snap of your fingers. The key to success is to determine your personal vision, have it fit within your home, respect its architecture, and stay within your budget. How do you begin this challenging process? And more importantly, how do you know what you don't know?

This book will guide you through the steps with information, photographs, and drawings from professionals, along with some personal stories from homeowners, who—like you—want a kitchen to match their style, cooking needs, and budget. We fondly refer to the profiles as **kitchen conversations**. They share the hows and whys in intimate detail, as if you are conversing with a friend or family member.

Why is kitchen design such a hot commodity now and on the tip of everyone's tongue? In recent decades, the kitchen has gradually become the heart of the house. Back in the 1950s, and even into the '60s and '70s, it was primarily a place to cook and eat casual meals. Dinner itself and other festivities were enjoyed in an adjacent dining room.

Enter the glamorous 1980s and '90s that led to larger homes, which made the kitchen more of a showpiece as new materials, appliances, and technology began to emerge. More chefs and cookbook authors also became celebrities, often on a first-name basis. More than one work triangle surfaced in these bigger home kitchens because many homeowners added multiples of equipment, often because more family members became interested in cooking. Thanks to a tsunami of cookbooks, cooking classes, food blogs, and cooking TV shows, often with fierce competition, naturally we all want the latest cooking, serving, and cleanup implements, along with great food.

However, the single most significant influence causing the rise in the status of kitchens was a global pandemic. This officially entered our lives on March 11, 2020, when the World Health Organization declared that SARS-CoV-2 caused a virus called coronavirus or Covid-19 (hereafter referred to as "Covid.") Cause and effect were almost instantaneous. Fewer people ventured to grocery stores; they had food delivered instead if they could. Many wiped off delivered packages before opening them and washed their hands repeatedly at their sinks. Fewer people ate in restaurants even before many shuttered due to government restrictions and failure to keep staff. Social lives came to a halt and family members limited who could be in their pods. Suddenly, we all felt shut out of society and most of us hunkered down in order to stay well. Overnight, kitchens morphed into multipurpose family hubs where everyone gathered to work and study from home, pay bills, do art projects, charge smart devices, share about their day, and simply hang out when there wasn't much else to do.

With less money spent on commuting, travel, eating out, and other activities, homeowners spent more time indoors. At the same time, staying home and paring travel meant many people accumulated savings and turned to their surroundings to make them more functional, comfortable, and tonier. A groundswell of work on homes began as more people looked at their kitchens more critically and realized they wanted to refresh what was already there. This was a propitious time for many to hit the go button on the kitchen re-do they had long considered but couldn't afford. There was also the opportunity to be home while overseeing the project.

Homeowners looked around and calculated whether to do a minor update (change hardware and/or refresh paint colors, backsplashes, countertops) or a full facelift (take a kitchen down to its studs, open it up, and build it back up again—possibly in a new location within the house). The islands were too small for hanging out; some lacked ample seating and storage. Cabinets looked dated, sagged, and cramped. Appliances didn't chill or heat food fast enough nor have the highly touted, high-tech extras such as apps that could alert homeowners to when a roast was done or more milk was needed. Faucets still required turning and touching when suddenly nobody wanted the risk of exposure to another person's germs.

Homeowners drew up wish lists and contacted designers, architects, contractors, and other specialists. Although infection numbers have since waned due to vaccinations, boosters, mask wearing, and social distancing, Covid still hasn't disappeared completely. Kitchen remodels continue whether you want your dream kitchen for a primary, secondary, outdoor, or vacation-home workspace.

We want everything to be perfect in our new kitchens—the best layout and traffic pattern, lasting materials (even better if they're sustainable), correct island size, energy-efficient appliances, artificial and natural light, features that will help you age in place, and, of course, within budget. To achieve perfection, even for those kitchens only getting a cosmetic tweak, it takes hard, expensive, time-consuming work, asking the right questions, getting bids, lining up a work team, and being patient.

"The pace for remodels waned at times, but it still can be a challenge to find contractors and sometimes locate materials and equipment, even after the supply-chain disruptions and shortages," says Marina Case, principal designer at The Red Shutters in Hudson, New York, and Martha's Vineyard, Massachusetts. "Those challenges remain but not to the same degree. Inflation, however, has caused costs to rise more—even as much as thirty percent," she says. Yet, interest in remodeling remains high. People are not inclined to move right now because of the high interest rates. Instead, they are holding onto their homes and making them their own.

Prices will vary when you talk to architects, designers, contractors, or other tradespeople you hire. These variations equate to wildly different budgets and labor costs in various locations, which is why experts recommend multiple bids.

- *Remodeling* magazine's Cost vs. Value report in 2023 pegged a minor mid-range kitchen redo at around $26,790, and an upscale major overhaul at about $154,483.

- Houzz, a highly respected online design and remodeling source, put the median spend on major remodels at $50,000, and minor redos at up to $14,000 in 2023.

- The US kitchen industry's main trade association, the National Kitchen & Bath Association (NKBA), reported in its *2023 Design Trends* report that the average cost of a large kitchen (350+ square feet) build or remodel is $130,000, with 29 percent spending $150,000 or more, which includes materials and labor. [To see the recent 2024 report, visit the NKBA website, www.nkba.org.]

The big price swings relate to the size of the room; whether the footprint changes; whether materials and appliances are selected or reused; whether glitches arise (such as a gas line needing to be relocated or electrical wiring needing an upgrade according to building codes); and all the labor costs.

Overall, everyone who undertakes a kitchen improvement thinks it's worthwhile and quickly forgets the temporary hardships—almost like childbirth! This is due in huge part to the influx of exciting new concepts highlighted in kitchen blogs, reality TV shows, kitchen showrooms, and home improvement stores.

NEW KITCHEN CONCEPTS

- Bigger, less visible, back of the house pantries
- More auxiliary spaces, such as at-home bars—a direct result of people learning to mix cocktails and mocktails during the Covid pandemic
- Outdoor kitchens to enjoy freshly prepared food, fresh air, and nature
- Better lighting to perform tasks and create moods
- Longer-lasting sustainable materials that conserve Earth's resources
- High-tech gadgets using apps, voice-activation, hand waving, and face recognition
- Fun, personal touches such as banquettes that resemble a 1950s-style diner with seating, and bold-colored appliances
- Built-in storage and spas for pets

How much to spend with resale in mind might spur debate, though kitchen dollars have been deemed well worth spending as more buyers look for "move-in ready" houses. Not everyone wants to spend time doing renovations, and others simply can't find the necessary work staff.

There's no happenstance when designing a kitchen. Careful planning and design require input from experts and homeowners who have done so successfully and turned their rooms into a hub of comfort, convenience, and personal self-expression. There are so many different options and opinions—from which countertops are most durable to which backsplashes won't be outdated fast—and even the continued value of that heart of the kitchen: the island. So many people make it their No. 1 wish list item, while others have begun to prefer a table instead of an island; one that may serve the same purpose yet offer a more personalized, comfortable place to eat. Such changes happen often.

This is our shared conversation. Please listen in.

CHAPTER 1

Inside & Outside the Boxes: Cabinets, Shelves, & More

Selecting cabinets is a complicated process, and one of the most significant decisions a homeowner can make when remodeling or building a kitchen.

Begin by looking at your budget. Cabinets represent the largest investment in the kitchen, but there are so many other related decisions to be made as part of the cabinet selection process. For example: what size/s do you need? What style of door fronts do you like? Do you want closed cabinets, open shelving, or framed glass doors? What type of material appeals to you, and what will work with the style of your home? You might love teak because it's the epitome of sustainability, but it doesn't come cheap. There are other sustainable options, however. So, back to the drawing board. What about color? Can you mix and match hues on the perimeter and island, if you have room for that feature?

Cabinet selection basically boils down to this: what you decide becomes a balancing act between budget, space, function, and aesthetics. If you're improving on an existing kitchen, there's also the cost of removing the old cabinets that adds to the overall budget for installing new cabinets. It's not the cost of the cabinets alone to consider.

Besides cost, function should rank high on your list. Most of us have accumulated stuff through the years to keep within the cabinets—or boxes, the industry term. You may want to put items within closed cabinets with solid doors, hidden away like a secret agenda. Open shelves (in a material that contrasts with the cabinets) above countertops in the main kitchen is a desired look to give the kitchen a modern, updated aesthetic. You may also want to store items that don't need to be seen or aren't used daily in the walk-in pantry, known under a number of other names such as "dirty kitchen" or "scullery." The key is to put away what you don't use frequently rather than crowd counters, where you want unobstructed places to work.

Next, when deciding on the cabinetry's construction, consider its design—door style, material, finish, color, and hardware, hinges and pulls. This is no easy task because, once again, there are so many options and huge price ranges within each category.

Opposite Smallbone kitchen cabinetry is repainted to appear more like lacquer in this kitchen by director of interior design, Jessica Shaw, from The Turett Collaborative: Architects & Interior Designers.

CLOSED CABINETS

Closed cabinets come in three main types, which means there are different costs associated with your new kitchen cabinets. The varying costs depend on what type of cabinet you select.

Stock cabinets

At the entry-level cost and most affordable, stock cabinets are the equivalent of off-the-rack clothing that cannot be altered or hemmed. They come in limited sizes. Standard heights for upper cabinets are 30, 36, and 42 inches and, for bridge cabinets— those over a refrigerator or above the hood vent above the range—standard heights are 12, 15, 18, and 24 inches. Depth is 12 or 24 inches and width is nine, 12, 15, 18, 24, 30, 33, and 36 inches. Base cabinets may run 34.5 inches high without the countertop or 36 inches with the countertop, and tall, pantry-type cabinets run 84, 90, and 96 inches.

Stock cabinets are usually made of affordable wood and composite wood materials or particle board and come in limited paint colors and finishes. What you see is what you get. The advantage is that you usually can order and get them delivered fast—sometimes in a matter of days, depending on sizes and number of cabinets needed. For places to shop, think retailers like IKEA or big-box stores like The Home Depot or Lowe's.

Suzan Wemlinger of Suzan J Designs, Decorating Den Interiors, in Milwaukee, Wisconsin, says a good stock option is a plywood box, which is essentially made of thin sheets of wood glued together to form a single sheet. "These are solid, durable, and paintable but cost less than solid wood. A step down and more affordable might be a medium density fiberboard (MDF), which is sustainable for it contains recycled wood fibers and resin. Because costs vary based on market conditions, it's always good to compare prices."

Linda Reiner, a design consultant to Kitchen Magic in Nazareth, Pennsylvania, adds other stock options to the possibilities such as a half-inch pressboard cabinet with vinyl-shrink wrap doors on MDF or more expensive, three-quarter-inch birch plywood. Both are dependable choices. If you buy off the shelf, there are no alterations or customization options. However, if you start considering modifications you want to make to a possible stock cabinet choice, such as changing dimensions so they will fit better into your kitchen plan or function better for how you plan to use them, stock cabinets probably aren't the right choice, says Jodi Swartz, owner of KitchenVisions outside Boston, Massachusetts. When that's the case, she recommends stepping up to semi-custom or even custom, depending on budget.

Semi-custom cabinets

These cabinets come in more sizes so there's more flexibility in getting the exact dimensions desired—going up to the ceiling or fitting them into an awkward-shaped corner. They are also generally available in more colors, finishes, wood species, and styles, and may even be more durable. The downside is that they typically cost more than stock cabinets, and they take longer to fabricate.

Opposite White-painted wood cabinets on the top and bottom with touch latches are mixed with rift-cut white oak ones in between, which flank a range to add warmth to a pristine space designed by Eddie Maestri, AIA, Maestri Studio.

The reeded glass storage cabinet is more like an architecturally influenced furniture piece than a utilitarian cabinet.

Open storage is installed near the large window with wooden shelves to add warmth.

The dining room and kitchen work in sync to create an upscale look, with reeded glass in front of shelves to simulate a black-framed window.

Following pages Frameless cabinets from Eclipse Cabinetry anchor the warm contemporary flavor of this kitchen designed by Monica Lewis, CMKBD, MCR, UDCP, and Brittany Miller, both from J.S. Brown & Co. The frameless construction gains 1.5 inches of access opening in each cabinet, and the TFL (thermally fused laminated) slab doors in Arizona Cypress finish can be wiped clean in a flash. Contrasting finishes give interest to the sleek design and help the kitchen blend with stained wood finishes found throughout the home.

The timeline to receive semi-custom cabinets varies greatly, so it's best to check with the kitchen showroom or your kitchen designer to find out how long it will take. Semi-custom cabinets are similar to buying a suit off the rack, but then having it altered to fit you just right.

Custom cabinets

These are the equivalent of couture. They are the most expensive option and may take many months to be manufactured. However, it's worth the wait to gain the exact size, style, and shape you need, or a preferred finish or color—even a custom mixed color, wood species, or exotic veneer. Adding some desired customization within the boxes for built-in knife or spice racks can be done at the cabinetmaker rather than inserting aftermarket items. Swartz recommends custom when a homeowner wants a built-in "library effect" of full walls of cabinetry that are ganged together to alleviate seams. These can be installed in one piece, usually on-site.

The key is to see what's available, which is the best way to gauge what you like, what you can afford, and what fits (as much as possible) into your desired timeline. To start, head to a big-box store. There, right before your eyes, will be dozens of examples. Next, visit specialty kitchen or cabinet shops. Each will showcase a wide variety of styles and colors. Look carefully at door styles, colors, finishes, types of wood you like—perhaps a plain slab door or one with raised or recessed panels.

Do your research. Before your visit, compose a list of questions to ask the kitchen professional. Ask about the materials used, the construction, the finishes, and how they are applied. What is the composition of the outside and inside of the box? Is it made from hardwood or a composite such as MDF or less expensive particleboard that is made of wood chips, or perhaps a wood veneer? Such details will factor into the box's durability and price. Is the finish catalyzed, one that hardens to become stronger as it cures? Can you modify the existing door styles they offer? Ask each retailer or manufacturer the anticipated length of durability, which, of course, also depends on the frequency of a product's use. Keep in mind that an older couple who barely cook at home may be able to have certain cabinets for years; a young couple with children who aren't as careful may need repairs along the way.

CONSTRUCTION

On another note, find out whether the cabinet is fabricated as an inset, full, or partial overlay door style. Inset doors are set into the cabinet frame and fit flush with the cabinet face when closed. To open requires a pull or knob. Hinges can be concealed or exposed, but most often are concealed for a cleaner look. Inset doors cost more than overlay doors in part because of the exacting nature of the fabrication to get a perfect fit of the door into the opening. The opening is then slightly smaller on this cabinet door style because of the construction.

Full overlay doors look similar to inset doors. They cover the cabinet face but are not set inside the cabinet frame. They provide slightly more storage within.

Partial overlay doors have a space between the two doors of the cabinet that shows a strip of wood (called the stile) so, unlike the full overlay doors, the partial overlay doors do not meet in the middle. This is the least expensive option of the three.

Materials used inside the box may differ from outside and help to pare costs, although if it's less sturdy, it may not wear as well. The most widely used materials are MDF, plywood, and particleboard with melamine—and, sometimes, stainless steel. Reiner recommends that the shelves within should ideally be installed as adjustable so you can rearrange for different contents.

Look at the hinges and drawer slides to see how easily doors and drawers open. Some self-closing hinges (called self-close) have a spring built in so when you start to close the cabinet door, the spring takes over and pulls it closed. Some doors may just require a tap to open; others may need a knob or pull. Swartz recommends that even a stock cabinet have a full extension soft-close drawer glide and a soft-close door to help extend its life.

FINISHES & WOOD SPECIES

The finish on the cabinet box and door front, and whether it's painted, stained, laminated, lacquered, veneered, or clear coated natural with wood grain showing through, are additional choices to make and will affect the final cost. At different times, one look and even one species may be more popular, but because you are likely to have cabinets a long time, you should choose what appeals to you and what will integrate into your home's aesthetic and architecture rather than what's on trend at the time.

Popular woods today are maple, white oak, hickory, birch, and alder. Some work better left natural or with a light stain; some can be painted or lacquered. Currently, natural wood is popular because of the overall trend of more natural colors and organic materials, borrowed from Scandinavian or Danish design. It's a look that many think benefits health and wellbeing.

Even if a cabinet appears natural, there is most often a finish applied—perhaps a wash, glaze, tint, or ceruse, a technique that creates somewhat of a two-tone effect to bring out the grain in oak. "To get a certain cabinet look that appears to have no stain, the grain of the wood is important," Wemlinger says. White oak, especially quarter sawn, has become popular, in part because of the variation in its grain and how it accepts finishes. Rift-sawn white oak is another option but is more expensive. For a painted cabinet, Wemlinger favors maple, poplar, or sometimes alder because of their smooth finishes.

Swartz's firm also uses a lot of white oak as well as walnut veneers, and, with either, prefers to apply a stain. MDF, maple, and birch, however, are painted. Painted cabinets were once more expensive than wood, but now both are similar in price. And because of supply-chain challenges, currently MDF is less expensive than plywood but that could change. Prices also depend on location. Wood is now plentiful in southern states and Canada. The cost is increasing almost everywhere, along with shipping, so buying local is smart—and sustainable.

To determine what cabinet door style, wood, finish, and color is most likely to appeal in their home, many homeowners ask to borrow a door sample or two and "live" with them for a while to make the best decision.

Marina Case generally prefers a Shaker or simpler style cabinet front. "They are more timeless and easier to keep clean," she says. When it comes to choosing the cabinet color or finish, she advises taking your time. "It's the most important decision you will make because you will have to live with it for many years. While white is the most timeless in general, there are several paint shades in greens and blues that I also like."

CABINET MEASUREMENTS

To get cabinets to fit within a layout, measurements are taken for the entire room, then the cabinet plan is drawn, and the sizes of boxes are determined. Besides having cabinets align evenly in a row, the measurements help determine the length of the material needed for countertops (and the seam placement) and the square footage of tiles, amount of paint, or number of wallpaper rolls for the backsplash, and areas in between the countertop and upper cabinets. You don't want your designer ordering too much more of anything than is required, though it's standard practice to order up to 20 percent more of tile, which allows for accidents, breakages, and pattern matching, and enables you to keep stock aside if your tile becomes discontinued. Likewise, ordering extra wallpaper will help prevent similar issues from delaying the project. The contractor or designer also determines how many pulls and knobs are needed, with a few extra purchased for the same reasons.

This spread Remodeled to meet the needs of a multigenerational family, this kitchen has multiple seating spots and a large island of clear cherry cabinets, with walnut inlays with similar cabinetry around the perimeter of the room, painted white for contrast.

A breakfast bar is concealed from view when not in use but, when open, the wooden pull-out shelf makes prep easy.

Floor plans and elevations show how designer Wendy Johnson, CMKBD, Designs for Living by Wendy LLC, added multiple areas to work, cook, clean up, and congregate.

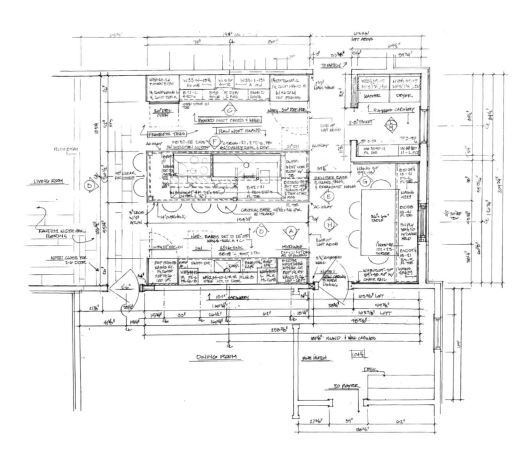

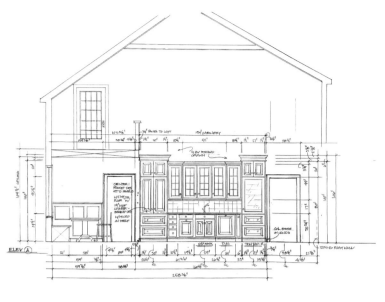

WORKABLE CHEF'S KITCHEN WITH VINTAGE FARMHOUSE CHARM

In conversation with Colleen, St. Louis, Missouri

Colleen, a private caterer and catering director in St. Louis, Missouri, wanted a chef's kitchen in her vintage 1914 frame farmhouse. The kitchen hadn't been updated since 1994, when Colleen and her husband Charles first moved in. Colleen wanted a simple, efficient layout that would be durable, stain resistant, and allow for easy food prep like a top-notch working restaurant kitchen. At the same time, she and Charles wanted the space to be comfortable and inviting, and to match the décor of their rustic home.

Here are some of the changes Colleen made:

► Installed new cabinets that go up to the 10-foot-high ceiling, which are extra deep with metal slots to hold all of Colleen's hotel/oversized pans and cutting boards, with roll-out shelves.

► Added vintage-looking, raised, circular, brushed-brass knobs.

► Replaced the tile countertops with a honed, beveled granite in ivory, brown, gray, and black tones.

► Added a baking station with four electrical outlets and a granite countertop to the left of the sink. Several drawers underneath hold all baking utensils such as pie plates, rolling pins, cake pans, and more.

► Replaced the old oven and range with a five-burner Bosch gas cooktop, so Colleen can cook several items at once. Over the cooktop is an ivory-colored wood hood with a metal insert vented to the outside.

► Added an oversized, stainless-steel double Bosch oven big enough for large pans. One oven is both a convection and regular oven and the other is a regular oven.

► Exposed the brick chimney, which has open walnut shelving for Colleen's extensive cookbook collection and, on the other side, a double-door, floor-to-ceiling pantry with self-closing drawers so Colleen can pull them out and view ingredients.

► Designed an island by taking an antique, handmade piece of furniture, adding wheels, and putting on a new solid walnut top that is treated with butcher block oils to make it safe for food preparation.

► Took down five feet of a wall to increase the footprint of the kitchen.

► Added overhead and undercounter lighting.

► Put in an undermounted chef's sink; the old sink had a lip and was difficult to keep clean. One side of the sink is huge for washing oversized cookware and the other side is smaller and has a garbage disposal.

► Installed a single-handle gooseneck Kohler faucet.

► Opted for an oversized, stainless-steel GE double-door fridge with a pull-out freezer door underneath.

Budget: $30,000–$35,000

Actual cost: More than $40,000

Timeline: Five months

Professionals involved: Colleen hired friends, a local contractor and his wife, and a kitchen designer instead of an architect.

Best feature: The exposed brick chimney and how it frames the pantry and the double oven.

What sets it apart: It's a vintage-looking but brand-new "cook's kitchen." Colleen says she's no longer shuffling food from one oven to another.

Regrets: None

Lesson(s) learned: "Make sure you want to do a kitchen gut renovation before you commit to it. It's a long-thinking process, a mess, and is expensive," Colleen says.

Above (left) Blending the warmth of stained walnut cabinets, stainless-steel framed glass doors, and gray perimeter cabinets creates layers of texture and color in this kitchen designed by Morgante Wilson Architects, based in Evanston, Illinois.
(right) In another project, Morgante Wilson Architects chose cerused white oak cabinetry for the island and incorporated steel accents to add warmth and texture to this classic white kitchen.

THE CLIMATE EFFECT

Do a weather check. The location of the home should also be factored in since water and humidity or extreme heat or cold may affect wood and finish selections. When it comes to humidity and moisture, wood and water do not mix. "If there is consistent water contact with wood cabinets, mildew could develop and wood could warp," Reiner says. Even where the cabinets are placed in the kitchen can influence how well they hold up. Reiner advises always putting at least 30 inches of space between a range top and the underside of the cabinet above it to prevent it from catching on fire.

Swartz agrees. "In a very humid area, a painted cabinet's stile and rails may split over time or joints may loosen. In a cold area with heat on or in warmer weather, wood contracts, then expands," she says. For these reasons, white oak, natural cherry, and light woods such as birch and maple work well in any climate if stained. This also makes them easier to maintain than paint. Textured laminates or very dark wood, like a charcoal gray or espresso-colored stain, can be very forgiving. Swartz recommends keeping a home's climate controlled with consistent temperature settings (heat or air conditioning) to help stabilize the wood. MDF boxes and doors/drawers tend to have fewer separation problems with temperature changes than many woods.

UP TO THE CEILING OR NOT

There's no rule of thumb about going up to the ceiling or leaving space in between the top of cabinets and a ceiling. While standard cabinets are 30, 36, and 42 inches high, extra-tall cabinets can be 48 inches and good for storing items not used daily. Many extend them to the ceiling to increase cupboard space. This design decision also lends itself to a cleaner, more updated look, which also includes long, elegant stainless-steel pulls.

Sometimes a decision for the height is made based on whether the ceiling is slanted or uneven. Swartz likes to go to the ceiling, if possible, to get the extra storage. She also knows how to compensate when ceilings are uneven, but this is a question worth asking your design professional.

Left Crisp white cabinetry is paired with contrasting open shelving in this kitchen designed by Sindhu Peruri, Peruri Design Company, Los Altos, California. Extending cabinetry to the ceiling draws your eye upward and creates a seamless look. Architecture by Architecture Allure Inc.

Opposite Frameless cabinetry in horizontal grained bamboo veneer and high-gloss white lacquer houses LeMans' corner pull-outs, and bi-fold doors above that open with the touch of a finger. Designed by Danielle Florie, Bilotta Kitchen & Home, with Taylor Viazzo Architects

Above (left) Bilotta Kitchen & Home designed this kitchen that includes a deep, natural walnut drawer to perfectly fit pots and pans, with a divider to neatly stack lids and reduce clutter. **(right)** Sarah Barnard Design uses custom drawer inserts to accommodate knives, silverware, and other cooking tools for efficient workflow.

Following pages Bilotta Kitchen & Home features its own custom cabinetry, painted in Farrow & Ball's Railings color; open walnut shelves with LED lights over the sink; a white vent hood; and glass-front wall cabinets.

DOORS OR DRAWERS & WHAT'S WITHIN

Many designers advise using drawers beneath the countertop for one easy motion rather than having cabinet doors that must be opened first and then shelves pulled out. Within any cabinet or drawer, organizational systems can make them more functional, whether they are pegs to keep dishes in place, racks for spices or knives, trays for cutlery, slots for trays, and lazy Susans for hard-to-reach corners. Homeowners may want some drawers made extra deep—or high—for larger items like casserole dishes, pots, and pans.

More expensive custom cabinetry often comes with these features included, but there are countless options available online and in stores such as The Container Store, Rev-a-Shelf, The Home Depot, or Lowe's. They should be added into cabinets near their point of use; for example, cutlery and glasses stored near a dishwasher, and pots and pans near a range or oven.

It is important to know what you need before you invest in these systems since costs can quickly climb. Keep in mind what you would traditionally store in your cabinets before heading to a store or making a purchase, as opposed to buying organizing systems first. Planning the storage and usage ahead of time is key to well-functioning kitchen cabinets.

Finding storage

Even when it seems there's not going to be enough storage in a kitchen, a good designer often becomes a detective and finds surprising possibilities. Wemlinger often takes a small closet in or near a kitchen that does nothing but hold stuff on a few shelves and reimagines it as a pantry for canned and dry goods. "With the right design, it can hold all food essentials, leaving the main cabinetry for dishware, flatware, pots, and pans." Swartz has moved walls if necessary. She has also added appliance garages on countertops in corners, to keep smaller appliances out of view when not needed.

MIX & MATCH

These days, you can color your choices in lively mixes. While white kitchens remain the most popular among buyers, color has made inroads. It's a very personal decision to introduce a hue or two into your cabinetry. Some homeowners use one color on perimeter cabinets and a different one on base cabinets of an island, if one is included in their design, or they might mix up colors even on perimeter cabinetry, putting the darker hue below to add an anchor to the design. They may also tie together the varied palette by using countertops of the same color and style throughout. Mixing both painted and stained cabinets within one kitchen gives a striking look when executed correctly.

Below Open shelving and closed cabinets with two contrasting finishes—light wood (natural elm) and high-gloss white lacquer—give this Snaidero kitchen by 210 Design House a sense of spaciousness, warmth, and contemporary charm.

Opposite Nicole Ellis Semple, AIA, Semple + Rappe Architects, maximizes storage in this small U-shaped kitchen. Custom cabinets made locally from maple plywood have a flush overlay door, with MDF fronts painted green to match backsplash tiles, and oak handles.

REFINISHING OR REFACING

Cabinet costs can be cut dramatically if existing cabinets are in decent condition. Perhaps the style still appeals and the fronts can be removed, sanded, cleaned, primed, painted or sprayed, and refinished rather than replaced. It is still recommended to use a professional painter or contractor skilled in this type of work. This process saves spending money on a totally new box and is a highly sustainable practice. A less invasive process is to have the doors removed and repainted, either on- or off-site, then reinstalled—though sometimes painted doors may not wear as well, depending on the process used. For those who don't like the style of the door but want to retain the rest of the box, the front can be replaced or refaced with an entirely new door.

OPEN SHELVES

One trend that is gaining more popularity in recent years is the use of open shelves above countertops rather than having a row of boxes with door fronts. The look allows for some breathing room and more light in the kitchen and also permits homeowners to display some of their most frequently used crockery, and glassware, or best-looking cookbooks and collectibles. Shelves also cost far less to construct and install than the typical cabinet and can be made of a different material, such as wood or stainless steel, for some visual diversity. The downside of open shelves is that they can become big dust collectors and messy looking if items on display are not arranged neatly. Homeowners leaning toward this option should decide how willing they are to spend time tidying up.

REPAINTING CABINETS & OTHER INEXPENSIVE TWEAKS

In conversation with Lucy and Steve, Baltimore, Maryland

This thirtysomething couple with two young children never thought their first home, a new townhouse where they had been living for six years, would be their forever home. They found their galley kitchen to be aesthetically displeasing and wanted to make changes, yet they reasoned: why do an expensive renovation when they might move at some point in the near future? They came up with a smart solution: change what bothered them the most without spending a bundle.

The tipping point to tackle this project was the pandemic, when they were stuck at home. Not only were they preparing all meals (instead of just breakfast and dinner), but they were spending almost all of their time on the level of their home with the displeasing kitchen, living room, and dining room. They gave up restaurant eating and, for a period, Lucy and Steve cooked elaborate, themed dinners for at-home Saturday date nights. They also added some new endeavors such as baking a challah weekly and trying their hand at bagels. "We were cooking so many meals that we grew to dislike the kitchen more," Lucy says.

Lucy and Steve changed the dark, wood cabinets that looked old, tired, and dated; unattractive hardware; the lack of a tile backsplash, which meant the walls were splattered; the yellow color of the existing walls; and a faucet that kept malfunctioning but which they had avoided replacing.

Once Lucy and Steve knew they didn't want to replace the cabinets, Lucy researched the repainting option. Their painter said he'd done such work before. They chose a Benjamin Moore white, which would make the galley space—open at each end to other rooms—look larger. At the same time, it made sense to change the pulls to something with more flair. At first, they considered gold, which had become popular. However, after talking to a few designers, they felt a dark gray would appeal to them and future buyers more.

To lighten the walls and make them work better with the gray in the dining and living rooms, Lucy and Steve went with a slightly different, lighter hue. Before painting, they decided on a subway tile in a glossy gray that would be practical, reflect light, and update the space.

And for a new faucet, they went with a contemporary design, in a deep charcoal, which Steve installed himself.

All the changes achieved their goal of giving the space a big facelift for a modest sum. "It's not our dream kitchen, but it's certainly much better looking. We don't dislike the space now," Lucy says.

- -

Budget: As little as possible.

Timeline: Six months (mostly due to pandemic-related delays and scheduling). The backsplash was installed in two days. Cabinets and walls were painted six months later.

Professionals involved: Cabinet and wall painter; tile installer.

Best feature: "The room is brighter and appears to be slightly larger," Steve says.

Regrets: "In theory, we wish we could have replaced the speckled granite countertops, too, but we knew that would prove too expensive for a kitchen that we don't plan to have forever," Lucy says.

Lesson(s) learned: "We wish we had done the changes sooner. I also learned to trust my design instincts. I asked a lot of people for their opinions and had a hard time deciding on colors and tiles. However, in the end, we made the decisions and like what we chose," Lucy says.

CHAPTER 2

Surfaces: Countertops, Floors, & Backsplashes

Major surfaces such as countertops, backsplashes, and flooring are some of the choices that give a kitchen its own personal stamp. A big part of the challenge when making choices for your surfaces is deciding how much of a starring role you want each to play. Is their main purpose to provide a focal point with a bold pattern or color or to act as an understudy to cabinets, appliances, walls, and ceilings? If the cabinets have a novel palette or material, if the appliances make a statement because of their oversized dimensions, or if a color is your inspiration, rather than traditional stainless steel, white or black, you may want surfaces to be more subdued. Designer Jodi Swartz likes to say, "There can only be one or two 'pink flamingoes' in a kitchen."

Whatever the material or color, your chosen surfaces must be durable and able to withstand regular everyday use—such as cutting at counters and an island; walking on floors in all sorts of shoes; wear and tear from pets; and water and grease splatters on walls. Even if they aren't eye-catching or the first thing you notice when entering the kitchen, any of these surfaces can still look handsome and fresh. In fact, some subtle yet lovely choices will keep a kitchen from looking dated. It is important to understand that experts may disagree about the maintenance and durability of certain materials, so make sure you do your own research and feel comfortable with your choices.

COUNTERTOPS

Many kitchen designers recommend first picking the countertop material, which can be the same or different from what goes on an island, if you have that feature. With surfaces today, you have myriad choices that vary in durability, price, sustainability, and edge treatment. The countertop surfaces may require visible seams since most are only available in limited widths and lengths. They may also require careful matching of patterns, known as bookmatching. The choice of an installer who is accustomed to working with various materials, particularly cutting them, is another important decision. Most stone yards work with multiple fabricators, who make a countertop template and then install the materials. Inquire about the availability of experienced installers and view their work before choosing one.

Opposite Jacob Laws, Jacob Laws Interior Design, uses layered textures in this kitchen, including an artisan oxidized brass sheet-wrapped peninsula; unfinished hardwood floors; honed black granite on countertops and the range wall; and a chiseled stone hood.

Following pages The smaller scale 'hive' pattern on these backsplash tiles creates a striking design with added texture. Their faint blue outline also provides a pop of color and contrast. The unique taupe and blue-grey veining on the marble countertops blends well with the kitchen's blue-and-white color scheme. Designed by Alexis Ring, Alexis Ring Interior Design, San Francisco, California. Architecture by Jeffrey A. Eade

In addition to the cost of the material, consider where it's coming from since imports from overseas—China, India, Italy, and Brazil—may cost more than domestically manufactured ones, largely due to shipping costs. They may also not be as readily available depending on what's happening with that country's supply pipeline, which was challenged during the Covid pandemic. Moreover, what happens if any of these materials arrive damaged? You may need to wait longer for a correction or make a fast switch. A good rule of thumb these days is to shop local, which also comes with the advantage of seeing and touching possible options and taking samples home to see in your space.

How novel you want to be is also a factor. Some homeowners are quite content with old favorites like concrete, a solid surface, granite, or laminate while others want something less common. Be aware that trends change—not overnight, but gradually. For example, granite, once highly sought after, has become so ubiquitous that many homeowners turn up their noses now at the thought of using it. Newer porcelain materials, which first mimicked woods and were used on floors in planks and tiles, are now replicating marble in a closely related version known as sintered stone. These materials are manufactured using new technology processes and are catching on because they're so versatile and resistant to fading, Swartz says. Another new look, called countersplash, was first used in Europe and is showing up more often. The countertop choice is repeated along the adjacent wall backsplash for an almost seamless look. "It makes quite a statement to take a veined stone and match the grain, from a horizontal surface, applying it vertically as a backsplash," Swartz says. But she warns: "Depending on the cooking surface, some stones can't be applied behind a cooktop or range."

Any choice should also factor in maintenance. Some surfaces need to be sealed periodically, like marble every three to six months, or like granite every few years, while others such as porcelain, laminate, engineered quartz, and sintered stone might rarely or never need upkeep except for a good clean after heavy use, says Suzan Wemlinger. Swartz also adds in quartzite, concrete, and soapstone as high-maintenance options. Quartzite needs to be sealed, soapstone needs to be oiled, and concrete needs to be waxed, in some cases.

It is important to know about height, too. Counters are generally 35.75 inches to 36 inches high. (A dishwasher should be no more than 34.25 inches high.) "If clients want a thick counter, there are many ways to address it," says Swartz. "Cabinets would need to be reduced in height to handle a thicker counter and still be 'counter height,'" she says.

To choose wisely, visit kitchen showrooms, tile stores, stone yards, and importers to see what's available. Prices will vary widely and depend on the quality, availability/rarity, and thickness. Also, ask about installation costs since they may rival the cost of the material. Here are a few more pointers:

Granite, a natural stone, comes in a variety of qualities, colors, patterns, and prices. It's durable, hard, resists scratches, and withstands staining and etching, says Swartz. Because it's natural, it's sustainable and many variations are widely available. When choosing granite, know that it must be purchased and "tagged" from a stone lot, each slab cut from a larger block, and numbered one behind the other, she explains. One con is that it's available mostly in mid-tone to dark

colors and may need to be sealed. But Wemlinger says that some sealants offer years of protection. Corinne Corbett, a designer at ProSource® Hudson Valley Wholesale, Poughkeepsie, New York, says some sealants work for 15 years. Wemlinger recommends knowing the type of sealant being used so you can adhere to a proper maintenance schedule. In addition, depending on where the stone is quarried, Swartz says that some off-gassing might occur.

Quartzite, another natural material, is considered harder and more durable than most marbles but not as hard as granite or quartz (an engineered version). "One of my first choices is natural quartzite stone with a honed or leathered finish. It has the aesthetic benefits of a marble but is much more stain resistant," says interior designer Jennifer Robin of Jennifer Robin Interiors, San Anselmo, California. It is also highly heat-resistant, though no material is 100 percent safe, Swartz says, so avoid putting hot pots directly atop it. Because of its patterns, it looks best when bookmatched so the pattern or veining is carefully matched. Some of its cons are that it stains easily (wipe up spills quickly); absorbs moisture; can chip; is softer than granite and quartz; needs to be sealed; and may be more expensive than other materials.

Quartz, an engineered material, is available from numerous manufacturers such as Caesarstone and Cambria®. It's hard, antimicrobial, resistant to scratches, and doesn't have to be sealed. It won't crack under normal circumstances but might if excess heat is placed on the countertop. It also may resemble the patterns of marble, can easily be seamed, and cuts beautifully for mitered edges. Kitchen design consultant Linda Reiner prefers it to marble, which is porous and stains easily, and says quartz can look a lot like marble. Swartz contends that it doesn't look quite as real as natural stones, so view it as an alternative, not as a replacement. And now there are some slabs available at 135 inches by 78 inches, which can be larger than natural stones.

Marble offers a classic, gorgeous look that's available in many variations in veining and colors. Think of the statues in ancient Greece and Rome that still look fabulous centuries later. But those marbles aren't exposed to cutting and pouring wine over them. If you might freak out each time you pour a glass of chianti over a slab or squeeze a lemon and some acid lands on the marble and etches it, this material may not be for you. It also may crack. "Those who still want it should be prepared to pay to have it sealed often and periodically repaired and repolished," says Swartz. Corbett says some companies require clients to sign a waiver if they decide to go with marble to ensure they are aware of the pros and cons. Many professional chefs choose to have marble in their personal kitchens, knowing these imperfections that build up over time are a part of the charm, and look at it as adding character to their kitchens.

Stainless steel gives counters a restaurant pedigree and will wear well for years. Dings may appear, and some don't like the look of aged patina and signs of wear. It's best to hire a fabricator and installer used to working with it.

Laminates have come a long way since they appeared in the 1950s; nowadays they're available in more materials that mimic another such as wood, metal, and stone. They hold up well and are among the most affordable choices. But the downside is that many homeowners want a harder surface and something that conveys a more affluent look, as well as something more resistant to heat.

Also, "no matter how good the replication of other materials, it cannot pass for real wood or stone," says Wemlinger.

Solid surface such as Corian®, developed by DuPont in 1967, is composed of acrylic polymer and alumina trihydrate, and is considered durable, hygienic, and affordable. It is nonporous and easy to clean, but the downside is that it can be damaged more easily if hot pots are placed atop, and it's more susceptible to scratches than quartz and granite. On the other hand, it is easy to repair.

Butcherblock is used for entire countertops or sometimes sections. Different woods have been used, such as maple, cherry, walnut, and more novel bamboo, teak, wenge, hickory, and mahogany. There are three basic construction styles of butcherblock: edge grain, face grain, and end grain. If used as a cutting board, butcherblock can breed germs, so it's best not to cut directly on it and always clean it with water and soap. It should also be sealed regularly with oil.

Porcelain and **sintered stone** are incredibly durable. "Two sintered stones—Dekton and Neolith—are heat and stain resistant," says Sandya Dandamudi, president of GI Stone in Chicago, Illinois. Dekton comes in lots of textures from leathered to honed, matte to glossy, and can range in appearance from the look of natural quartzite to marble, slate, and metallic finishes. "It's a stunning material that can also be installed in outdoor kitchens and won't fade or soften in the sun," Dandamudi says. But there is one big caveat, she adds: "Creating Dekton (and Neolith) countertops, backsplashes, or flooring requires an experienced Dekton-certified fabricator and special machinery, so it can be hard to find those skilled in working with it. While porcelain and Dekton perform almost the same in durability, Dekton is slightly stronger," she says. It also offers more textures than porcelain. And Dekton, along with porcelain, is more expensive to fabricate when compared to quartz and natural stone. Yet, in the end, it can be a cost-effective choice considering what it delivers. Swartz adds that anyone liking these choices should look at the full range since there are others besides Dekton and Neolith.

Soapstone has become one of the most desired surfaces for its classic look. "Soapstone is a historically relevant, extremely durable material. It is acid, heat, and stain resistant. It can be oiled to renew its finish or left raw to produce a rich patina over time," says Robin. Wemlinger adds that it will acquire a patina over time, so anyone buying it should be okay with the look changing as it ages.

Concrete and glass fall into the sustainable category and many people like that concrete can be stained multiple colors and that glass reflects light and can be backlit. The downsides of each of these are that concrete can stain, chip, and need to be waxed, and that glass scratches. Wemlinger adds that cabinets used with concrete need reinforcement because of the weight of concrete and that the countertops may crack. Glass, while durable, can crack or chip and can be difficult to repair. "It also is not as environmentally friendly as one would expect with recycled glass, because of the manufacturing process," she says.

Whatever choice you make, know that you can mix and match. Some clients like to put quartz on perimeter surfaces and a more expensive, natural stone on an island as a way to mix high- and low-priced materials, and contrasting textures, says architect John Potter, AIA, NCARB, partner at Morgante Wilson Architects in Evanston, Illinois.

Opposite Katherine Shenaman Interiors designs a tropical-inspired Florida kitchen, mixing white cabinetry with a bleached cypress wood island, a durable Calacatta Gold-style porcelain countertop, and a Moroccan Zellige tile for the backsplash.
Following pages This kitchen in California wine country designed by Jennifer Robin, Jennifer Robin Interiors, features an attractive and durable soapstone countertop on the island and Taj Mahal granite for surrounding countertops to create a rustic yet glamorous feel. Robin selected textural honeycomb tile for the backsplash to add warmth and visual interest. Architecture by Karen Jensen, Jensen Architects

Finally, match the right edge to the right material. Among the most popular choices are a pencil edge, or eased edge, a 90-degree mitered edge, ogee with concave and convex arches, bullnose with its slightly rounded edge, and bevel with quarter inch, or quarter-inch edge, says Swartz. "As a design approach, 90-degree, mitered, waterfall edges are very popular now," she says. Multiple thicknesses are another option, from a half inch to three-quarter inch to one-and-a-quarter inch, and more.

FLOORS

Next consider the floor; though some designers like Tom Segal, principal at Kaufman Segal Design in Chicago, Illinois, like to start most room designs with the floor choice as an anchor. "We usually like a wide plank wood for the warmth in our projects in East Coast or Midwest homes, or stone floors in warmer climates. However, in kitchens, the most important thing to consider about the color of kitchen floors is how they go with the cabinets and countertop materials." Robin agrees. "For a more naturally inspired aesthetic, I recommend choosing flooring that is just slightly darker than the cabinetry. The tones should blend and blur nicely to avoid high contrast. If the home is more modern or elegant in style, I opt for richer darker colors," she says. Segal says that porcelain tile has recently become popular for the ease of cleaning. If you add a rug atop the floor, cleanability should play into the type of rug since a kitchen rug is more likely to experience spills.

Before you start looking, decide if you want your floor heated since some materials won't work with electric coils underfoot. Also consider whether you want it to be the same as what's in adjacent rooms, particularly if the kitchen is part of an open-plan layout. Today you have major choices, including antique floorboards; reclaimed, recycled wood; newer hardwood; and engineered wood in choices such as pine, white oak, reclaimed oak, hickory, walnut, beech, birch, chestnut, ash, maple, and cherry. Some are harder, such as white oak, and some are softer, like hickory, so factor that in too when deciding. Dark woods show more wear and tear, dust, and scratches than light-colored woods, which also help a kitchen appear brighter—and sometimes larger, says Chris Sy, president of Carlisle Wide Plank Floors in Stoddard, New Hampshire.

Generally, inlays and borders are passé—except in very traditional homes—and are rarely used in kitchens. There is also an increasing number of faux floor choices in porcelain planks or tiles, referred to as luxury vinyl tile (LVT) or luxury vinyl plank (LVP). Some resemble wood but today they also mimic ceramic tile, slate, and other materials. Swartz prefers to use these newer choices in basement kitchens, where they can withstand possible moisture, rather than upstairs in the main kitchen.

Each choice offers pros and cons. The advantage of many engineered woods—those that consist of multiple layers of hardwood veneers glued and pressed together to improve stability—is that they come in wider widths (up to eight inches) and longer lengths (up to six feet), Swartz says, and more colors than previously available. Generally, wider planks offer a modern aesthetic; narrower planks are more traditional. "Some designers suggest mixing widths

This spread Stephanie Wohlner, Stephanie Wohlner Design, brings together a textured clay tile floor with a browned, antiqued leather granite countertop, Calacatta Gold marble backsplash, Moroccan Zellige tile under the cabinet, and reclaimed beams along the ceiling. Designed with Doug Durbin, nuHaus; architect Erik Peterson, AIA, PHX Architecture; and builder Anthony Salcito, Salcito Custom Homes

Following pages This large space now has some statement elements thanks to Jacob Laws Interior Design, with its choice of oversized, classic black-and-white, honed marble check flooring to match the proportions of the kitchen, and honed Danby marble on the workspace and counters.

for a different, often more casual look, though the downside can be a busy appearance," says K. Tyler, another partner in interior design at Morgante Wilson Architects. Wemlinger prefers real wood over faux, but steers clear of real wood choices for kitchens when there are client concerns about maintenance, which most often occurs when there are children and pets in the home. She also recommends never putting different LVT wood-look floors in a room that is adjacent to another room that has real wood floors, since the differences can be jarring. No matter how good an LVT wood-look floor is, it will not look natural up against the real thing.

On the plus side, cork tiles and/or planks are made of natural material that is resilient, forgiving, and affordable. On the con side, ceramic tiles are hard and may make it tough for someone to stand on them for long periods; if objects fall on them, they may break easily.

Factor in the style of the kitchen and house. For kitchens in older homes, Wemlinger often prefers wood and seals it well. "It adds warmth and character," she says. For rooms where ceramic tile will look best, she favors larger format designs of 22-by-22-inch or even 12-by-24-inch rectangular tiles rather than smaller 12-by-12-inch patterns that used to be favored. She also likes going with new, more popular shapes such as hexagons, triangles, and freeforms.

The floor selection can be a blend in tone to the backsplash and countertop, or it can be a contrast in tone, again depending on what the desired outcome is. "If every kitchen photo you admire happens to have a dark wood floor, nothing you select for the other surfaces will give you the desired aesthetic if you choose a neutral square tile for the floor. When looking at inspirational photos, consider how the whole room makes you feel. Don't only look at the individual surfaces," says Wemlinger.

Having the right finish is critical, and the good news today is that many finishes dry quickly so homeowners don't have to vacate their premises for days. Few materials have volatile organic compounds (VOCs), so they're better for the environment and homeowner. Most prefinished floors use an ultraviolent (UV) cure urethane, which protects wood from water. To clean this type of flooring, experts recommend using a damp mop and a mixture of water with oil and vinegar. Cost should always be factored in since exotic woods can challenge budgets, as will some ceramic tiles from upscale manufacturers. And matching patterns of any material can add to the final cost because a larger quantity may need to be purchased to do so. It's also wise to purchase a larger quantity of most materials—usually 15 to 20 percent more than you need—in case any arrive damaged, the design gets discontinued, or a few tiles need replacing over time.

BACKSPLASHES

When not painting or wallpapering, the choice favored nowadays for the backsplash is often tile. Your chosen tile can make a huge difference and many choices have changed greatly from years past. Decades ago, patterns often proliferated such as baskets filled with fruit or landscapes that suggested Italy. In more recent years, skinny glass tiles in different hues were often laid in horizontal grids like brickwork. Yet, some tile choices have remained classics such as subway tiles in three-by-six-inch rectangles, often in white, then in other neutral hues such as cream, gray, and even navy and black; the finish can be glossy for a traditional look or matte for a modern aesthetic. More textures along with more handcrafted artisan versions have also taken off to add a more personalized look. Tiles have also become larger of late, with subway tiles in three-by-eight, four-by-eight, or even three-by-12-inch options, and often installed in novel vertical or diagonal rows.

Purchasing and installing tiles is not one of the more expensive tasks in completing a kitchen, so adding a new backsplash can give a kitchen a fresh look and with less investment than replacing countertops, cabinets, or appliances—especially if a total redo is not the plan. The result can steal the show if the choice is in a bold color or with a textured design. Whatever the choice, it's best to install tiles all the way up to the ceiling if possible, rather than just partially along a wall, to give the room a richer, more finished look. Also, be sure the choices made on style, color palette, patterns, and textures are all compatible.

And if tiled walls do not appeal, you can always choose a paint color, preferably in an eggshell finish, or a wallpaper since once again paper is making its way back into kitchens, though in new patterns rather than the dainty florals, stripes, and checks of the past. Some wallpapers mimic other surfaces such as brick or stucco and some are textured, which helps conceal stains and fingerprints. Many of today's designs are manufactured to make them easier to apply, wipe clean, and remove, all of which were headaches in the past that required great effort, a lot of time, and the right wallpaper expert.

THE BEST-LAID PLANS OF MICE & MEN ...

In conversation with Stephanie, Short Hills, New Jersey

In 2005, when she was pregnant, real estate salesperson Stephanie fell in love with a vintage 1929 Tudor that she was hell bent on buying and converting into a modern swan. The kitchen needed special attention.

Stephanie says that what started as a fairly simple reno is the classic story of how, as the proverb goes: "The best-laid plans of mice and men go oft astray." She hired a kitchen designer and architect to start making improvements immediately. Then, life got in the way. Her baby, a son, arrived early. Work stopped and Stephanie realized nothing less than a total redo would be satisfactory. However, the Great Recession of 2008 happened and, to be prudent, Stephanie put it all on hold.

After years of saving, the work resurfaced in 2018. This time, Stephanie had a far bigger plan in mind and a different aesthetic.

Here are some of the features of Stephanie's dream kitchen:

▸ Custom, high-gloss black cabinets with inset doors, soft-close, made in Pennsylvania for $50,000

▸ Appliances such as a Wolf six-burner range, wall oven and steam oven; new Sub-Zero refrigerator; Miele dishwasher, and Viking wine refrigerator, all for $30,000

▸ Shaw white ceramic farmhouse sink with polished nickel fixtures and hardware

▸ Danby white marble countertops and full-slab backsplash, with outlets hidden under the cabinets

▸ Center island with walnut marine finish top and cabinets beneath in a stained taupe-gray

▸ Automatic refuse and recycling bin that uses a toe touch to open

▸ Custom, stained-glass window instead of backsplash over cooktop for $900

▸ Beverage center with hammered nickel bar sink, and glass-fronted cabinets with antique mirror panel in rear

▸ Dispensers at both sinks for reverse osmosis water, with push button for disposal

▸ Juliska pendant lights over the island

▸ Walk-in pantry with wave glass French doors

▸ Large, arched opening to the dining room and an adjacent teen lounge

Actual cost: Triple the original estimate because work went beyond the scope of the kitchen to the lounge; a mud room; primary bathroom; upgraded electrical panel to 200-amp; new boiler; new central air conditioner; instant hot-water heater; newly planted gardens, and new garage.

Timeline: 18 months for all work; four months for the kitchen.

Professionals involved: Kitchen designer who is also an architect, a contractor, and a landscape designer.

What sets it apart: "The goal was to make it look as if it could have been original to the house's era of 1929, yet be highly functional, sleek, and elegant," Stephanie says.

Regrets: "I tried to donate the perfectly good, high-quality [original] kitchen to a charity, but it did not work out. Sadly, all went into a dumpster. Also, the choice of the ceramic sink, which crazed and required replacing," Stephanie says.

Lesson(s) learned: Stephanie learned to go for what you want because you hopefully aren't doing this a second time; however, she suggests that you "Plan, plan, plan ... I wish I had done better planning on choices like marble, which has scratched, and the sink ... Most of all, the point is to love where you live, and I do."

FIVE EXTRA TIPS
TO ACHIEVE A COORDINATED LOOK
from designers Jodi Swartz and Suzan Wemlinger

▶ Bring home samples. "It's important to have samples of all the different surfaces when making final selections—don't just work from photos. Have several samples of each surface so you can see the variations in each tile/plank, which are likely to occur. For countertops, it's important, particularly with natural stone, to view the actual slabs that will be used in your home. There is so much variation in pattern flow, as well as different shades of the same color. This will help you coordinate patterns and colors," advises Wemlinger.

▶ Mix and match. "Feel free to mix larger patterns with smaller ones. Solid counters with veined ones," Swartz says.

▶ Choose an inspiration color for the kitchen or dining spaces. Add it to the backsplash. "I am a fan of color in splashes and hardware; they are easier to trade out in a couple of years," Swartz says.

▶ Start with one area. "How one homeowner or designer starts choosing selections varies from person to person, or project to project. If you find a backsplash tile you love, use that as the jumping-off point and make it the star of the show. The countertops can then be more subtle or low key, so they don't take away from the tile," Wemlinger says.

▶ Too many stars spoil the show. "If you've been saving photos of kitchens with amazing countertops, however, start with that instead. In this instance, make sure the backsplash is the little sister to the countertop—more subtle. It doesn't need to be plain or boring, just not the showstopper that the countertops are. It's also important that the patterns are not too similar. If the countertop has a dramatic flow through it as mentioned, the tile can be a soft wash of color with subtle variations, or it can be a solid color or neutral," Wemlinger says.

Right Andrew Franz Architect combines simple materials with countertops of statuary marble from ABC Stone, a backsplash of Komon terracotta tiles by Made a Mano, a solid reclaimed rift red oak floor, and open shelves.

CHAPTER 3

Appliances:
Your Essential Helpers

Kitchen appliances represent an important and major portion of your budget. It is prudent to select the right brand with the functions, size, materials, controls, ergonomics, and unique features that will meet your wants, needs, budget, room, and lifestyle. Doing so will make food storage, prepping, cooking, and cleanup easier and more enjoyable. And don't forget looks—style, color, and finish choices matter, too.

Whether you are buying brand new for the first time or replacing existing appliances, pay attention to all the possibilities. This includes service availability as well, since appliances may need attention within the first few months for a variety of reasons, says Michael Feiden, vice president at Earl B. Feiden, a family appliance chain in upstate New York. "We hear from consumers all the time that they're advised to use an 800 number, but it's important to have someone provide ongoing in-person support," he says.

Today there's a vast range of choices—and prices, according to designer Suzan Wemlinger, who has extensive knowledge of appliances. Many manufacturers offer packages of multiple pieces for a coordinated look and sometimes at a reduced price when purchased at the same time. The biggest difference in price is between freestanding and built-in appliances, Wemlinger says. The built-ins provide a more seamless design, but they can be more expensive. Prices, which skyrocketed during Covid, have now settled down, though many are still higher than they once were, Feiden says. Besides the price advantage of buying a package from a single brand, doing so can make servicing simpler.

The choices can also make a difference in resale. Consider how much your kitchen may appeal to the next buyer—some may care about having built-ins with stainless-steel fronts and a gas range; others want an induction cooktop because it's more energy efficient.

It's great to ask other people's advice but not to exclusively rely on it. Wemlinger recommends doing your homework and thinking through how you'll use each appliance. For example, do you need extra freezer space because you cook ahead, or do you want a refrigerator with a bigger interior capacity or an air purification system because you only want fresh ingredients? You may also want a big oven (or multiple ovens) for elaborate holiday cooking.

Opposite Sub-Zero and Wolf appliances are great choices for consumers who want quality that will last. The refrigeration preserves food for longer, saving a homeowner money by not wasting food that spoils. Sub-Zero and Wolf's cooking appliances are also precise, giving consumers confidence in their creations. Kitchen designed by Nancy Jacobson, Kitchen Design Partners

There are so many bells and whistles available now, like an extra rack that folds down in dishwashers for washing the family crystal, or quiet settings to pare noise. Today, equipment often comes with apps to download to let you program cooking needs even when away from home. Want your refrigerator to tell you when it's time to reorder milk or juice? That's possible; however, will you use this feature? Feiden says many customers don't, and he suspects the features may be more useful for companies to log in and help consumers resolve problems.

If you care about a name brand and the status or quality it connotes and you can afford it, go for it. Get that glass-fronted, industrial-style refrigerator or brightly colored enamel range. If you're into retro style, buy a refrigerator and matching range in a '50s color, perhaps turquoise, and in a curvy shape that evokes the Sputnik era. Feiden recommends checking first whether you will be able to get the brand serviced locally. Whatever you put on your appliance wish list, know that most equipment lasts a long time. Get what you want the first time, because it's smarter than having regrets and then buying twice.

Websites about remodeling, design, and specific appliances, such as HGTV, Houzz, Remodelista, The Spruce, Bob Vila Home Improvement, and The Healthy Kitchen, and consumer sites such as Consumer Reports, are great resources. Visit a few appliance or kitchen design shops and big-box stores in person for additional information. Each store may stock different brands and offer different expertise. Ask for help. It's wise to test products if you can. For example, the Viking Cooking School offers cooking classes using its brands at its site in Greenwood, Mississippi.

Above New York City–based design-build firm Bolster collaborated with architect Michael Fasulo, AIA, LEED AP, principal at Rodman Paul Architects, to renovate a 1950s brick home in Astoria, Queens, New York. The comprehensive renovation involved converting the entire house from oil and gas heat to greener electric, featuring a kitchen range with an induction cooktop. The vibrant backsplash was created using a diverse selection of materials, including colorful porcelain tiles. Anna Karp from Bolster acted as the general contractor.

Also, make a list of what you liked—and didn't like—about your previous equipment. Some homeowners prefer French doors on a refrigerator, others want just one door; some want a freezer on the bottom, and others want it on the top. And some want a separate refrigerator or freezer drawer or a combination in an island, bar area, or butler's pantry to reduce traffic in the main work triangle. There's no single piece of equipment that's right for everyone but certain models will better fit your style, room, budget, and how you like to work more than others. Here are more specifics to consider but these are just the tip of the iceberg.

RANGES: OVENS & COOKTOPS, ALONE OR COMBINED

One of your first decisions when choosing a range is the type of fuel you prefer to use—or must use, in the case of a condo building or home heating system. Some new buildings or communities insist on the use of electrical appliances, as concern about fuel consumption and energy use continues to grow. However, some homeowners prefer cooking with gas. If there is no gas line in a single-family home, it may be possible to have one added. Before you shop, know that gas is measured in BTUs (British thermal units), while electricity is based on wattage.

And then there's the newer kid on the block—induction cooking, which depends on an induction coil to heat only the pan. It has gained favor because it's considered energy efficient.

Some experienced cooks have very definite preferences; others simply learn to adapt depending on what comes with their home. Learn to find your preference. One big change Wemlinger has noticed over the last five years is that microwaves are less in demand. "People still want them but not always in the main part of their kitchen," she says.

Key considerations:

▶ **What are the pros and cons of induction?** Induction is more environmentally friendly than gas or electric cooking, it cooks faster, and the cooktop is easier to clean, says Wemlinger. However, induction may cost more—as little as $200 but as much as $1,100 versus gas or electric, Wemlinger says. You may also need different cookware, and there's more of a learning curve to master it.

▶ **How much do you cook, and for how many people?** If you cook for a lot of people or do holiday entertaining, you may need multiple burners on a cooktop and multiple ovens beneath (or installed separately). You might not want to wait for each dish to cook because you hope to serve everything at once. Pay attention to the interior size of ovens because they vary greatly. And be honest about what you want. "Some homeowners don't cook much, but they still want a huge capacity in case," Wemlinger says.

▶ **Will your choices fit with your new kitchen layout?** When you go to look at stores and get closer to buying, bring along a copy of your kitchen plan, a rough sketch, and a tape measure to ensure appliance choices will fit in the proper places. The most typical size for a home range is 30 inches, but Wemlinger says they measure bigger, as large as 36 inches, 48 inches, and more. A La Cornue, a high-end glamorous model, can be six feet long, but comes in other sizes, too.

▶ **If there isn't room to fit a certain range, would it be possible to install wall ovens?** Wall ovens typically come in standard widths of 24, 27, 30, and 36 inches. Feiden recommends sticking with the same brand if you buy multiple ovens, especially if you want them located together. But if they're placed in different areas of the room, the size and even the brand don't have to match, he says.

It's a personal decision whether you go with a gas or electric wall oven. Wemlinger says most of her clients still favor gas because of how it cooks. Some homeowners want more than one oven and place them in different areas of a room, so multiple cooks won't get in each other's way. Be sure that a wall oven is placed at the right height, so the cook doesn't need to bend down low, especially as they get older, and be sure its door can be opened fully without banging into a cabinet. If young children are in the room, having the oven up higher can be smart to avoid accidents.

Previous pages and above
Anissa Zajac, House Seven Design, includes such custom L'Atelier Paris items as a Paris French stainless-steel range with six gas burners and walnut handles, Coup de Feu multipasta cooker, two large convection ovens, and dual working cabinet, and storage drawers on either side.

- ▶ **Do you have specialized cooking needs?** There are individual cooktops on the market that work well in small kitchens or for those who like to occasionally use a wok, grill, induction burner, or steamer as an auxiliary cooking accessory.

- ▶ **Do you have certain requirements because you're older or have a disability/physical limitation(s)?** Consider side-hinged doors on an oven and microwave at counter height to make them easier to open and avoid hunching over or lifting dishes over a hot oven door, says Rosemarie Rossetti, certified disability-owned business enterprise, certified living in place professional, and certified senior home safety specialist. (See Chapter 13.)

- ▶ **Do you like the look of a slide-in, wall-mounted, or freestanding range?** Some homeowners care greatly about the integrated look of a slide-in range; others are content with freestanding. "The choice is usually based on aesthetics and price," Wemlinger says.

- ▶ **Is a self-cleaning feature important to you?** This may hinge on how much you cook or what you cook—foods that splatter, such as duck a l'orange, can create a mess! A self-cleaning feature naturally adds to the total cost but is well worthwhile—especially as you age. "Most homeowners prefer a self-cleaning oven," Wemlinger says.

- ▶ **How important are the added extras?** Some are dazzled by these but debate whether they're necessary. Others seriously use them, so decide. Feiden ticks off some features that might appeal:
  - Big oven windows and good lighting to allow peeks at what's cooking
  - Temperature devices that can confirm certain foods, like a roast or turkey, are ready to eat
  - Porcelain racks for easier cleaning
  - Racks that slide in and out easily

- ▶ **Do you want digital technology?** Some want the latest; others want the simplest. Wemlinger says most of her clients prefer the simpler knobs.

- ▶ **Do you want to go with convection, another new darling?** Convection uses an internal fan to move air around, Wemlinger says, and adds that it can reduce rotation when multiple dishes are cooked on racks, offer quick preheating, and promote browning.

- ▶ **How much can you afford?** Set a budget. Think about your total appliance budget and set aside an amount for the range and/or ovens, which will represent a sizable chunk, along with your refrigeration choices. If you want a certain expensive oven, such as a La Cornue that can easily run beyond $13,000, you may need to cut back elsewhere. If you're feeling cash strapped, consider buying appliances as a package.

- ▶ **Are there additional cooking options to consider for an outdoor kitchen?** For an outdoor kitchen, you'll want to consider a grill—gas, electric, or wood pellet—and maybe a pizza oven and/or smoker. Factor in the climate and whether you'll want it constructed as part of a kitchen counter or as separate, freestanding pieces on a deck, terrace, or patio. (See Chapter 10 for more information.)

HOODS

Nobody wants to smell last night's dinner forever, especially when it's something like fish, brussels sprouts, or a spicy stew with lots of garlic. And certainly, nobody wants grease splatters all about.

Key considerations:

▶ **Which size is best?** Wemlinger says it should be at least as wide as the range or cooktop and offer enough cubic feet per minute (CFM) for the amount of BTUs in your range or cooktop. Some homeowners who don't have a hood have an exhaust fan vented to the outside.

▶ **Will it be noisy?** This may be important if you're trying to have conversations and don't want to yell. Many people do care about the noise level of a hood, so be sure to either ask or listen to it in action, if possible.

▶ **How chic should it be?** Hoods today are making a statement and many have become a wow factor in a kitchen. There are so many choices, with some resembling chimneys with the vent enclosed within and against the wall, while others may be over an island and drop down and rise up. Generally, there are five types available with vastly different aesthetics that are the driving force in choice. Wemlinger's big caveat: "Be sure the scale of the hood works in the room, so it doesn't overpower the space."

Above Appliances in this modern kitchen, designed by Susan Brunstrum, Studio Brunstrum, include a microwave drawer, inset gas cooktop with an oven below, two dishwashers flanking the island sink, and an under-counter beer fridge. All features support ease of use, cleanliness, and functionality.

Following pages Designer Nancy J Ruddy and the CetraRuddy team added a narrow-depth wall in this relatively compact apartment kitchen and incorporated space-saving solutions such as stacked wall ovens, a drinks trolley, microwave, and walnut cabinetry that conceals appliances.

MAKE IT MODERN, FUNCTIONAL, & THEATRICAL

In conversation with Sioux and Pieter, Hudson Valley, New York

When a young couple living in New York City looked for property to build a weekend home more than 20 years ago, they knew the kitchen would assume a starring role. "We both love to cook but also entertain very casually," says Sioux, who founded a technology recruiting firm with husband Pieter. They knew friends and family would gather routinely for their cooking adventures, during which everyone, including their teenage daughter, chips in.

The couple hired an architect schooled in modernism by the late I.M. Pei to design a curved, red cedar–clad house and bring their vision to life. Together with the architect, Sioux and Pieter:

- made the open-plan room equal parts kitchen, dining, and living, with the kitchen occupying the front;
- added a fireplace at the center of the house to offer a sense of separation;
- installed a five-burner Wolf cooktop on the oversized five-by-13-foot curved island so that the hosts and cooks can talk to guests sitting at stools or gathering around;
- used Absolute Black granite countertops on the large island, which required two slabs seamed together;
- arranged other appliances (refrigerator, dishwasher) on the back leg, with the sink facing the front yard;
- divided the workspace and formed a U-shape, but added a short peninsula leg;
- selected other quality appliances, including a Thermador double oven, without choosing the most expensive or luxe options;
- chose a flat cabinet in Spanish red lacquer from German-based manufacturer Poggenpohl; and
- lined the interior side of the island and a bar sink with cabinets, to mix drinks away from the cleanup zone.

Sioux and Pieter's teenage daughter has cooked in this kitchen since she was two years old. After standing on a stool to bake cookies, she is now comfortable making croissants, macaroons, and frosted layer cakes from scratch, and encourages her friends to join in, which they did over Zoom during the pandemic.

Making good appliance choices has ensured durability for 20 years and counting, which makes the space reliable and functional every day.

Actual cost: Over budget because of the expensive cabinets, but they've held up well for more than two decades.

Timeline: One year as part of the ground-up building project; the kitchen was installed in a day or two because the cabinetry was pre-made.

Professionals involved: Architect, designer, and contractor.

Biggest challenge: The curved countertop, which is so large it required a seam.

What sets it apart: The curves in the kitchen, which make for an elegant traffic flow as you enter the house and then move into the kitchen. The deep red of the cabinets really stands out against the white walls.

Best feature: The cooktop facing the countertop seating area, as well as the deep counter. The whole kitchen is spacious enough to have five or six people working together, cooking, and conversing. Sioux says the result is that "guests come [to] cook, talk, eat, and clean up together."

Regrets: Not installing a second dishwasher and using drawers under the island for knives, which are out of sight from children but not as easy to access when needed.

Lesson(s) learned: "Pay attention to how you live," says Sioux. "If you aren't a cook, don't install expensive equipment. Buy good brands but don't go crazy."

Opposite Sharon McCormick, Allied CT, AIA, Sharon McCormick Design, gives an outdated kitchen a functional layout for frequent entertaining, placing both a wine cooler and warming drawers close to the living and dining rooms.

- ▶ **Which materials are available?** The exterior these days may be modern or a restaurant-style stainless steel, old-fashioned wood, or traditional stucco, any of which may be selected because they match cabinetry or stand out and are different. Details may be incorporated; years ago, corbels and brackets were in, but a sleek look with iron brackets is now popular in a traditional kitchen, Wemlinger says. You may also opt for a look that matches your cabinetry.
- ▶ **Are there any smart features?** Smart range hoods can be controlled from a smartphone with an app that will start, stop, or adjust ventilation if you're slow cooking something, upstairs on the phone for a work call, or simply not at home.
- ▶ **How does venting work?** Preferably, you can vent to the outside, but if this is not possible, have a vent that gets rid of fumes and smoke by recirculating air inside the kitchen.

MICROWAVES

When microwaves first emerged, they sat on countertops looking clunky and taking up a large amount of real estate. Since then, more homeowners choose to have them built in above a range, below a countertop, or in a drawer.

- ▶ **Where's the best place to put a microwave now?** Inside a vented cabinet, Wemlinger says.
- ▶ **What else should it feature?** A convection feature offers two for the price of one.
- ▶ **What if we won't use it much?** Put it in a pantry if you have the space.
- ▶ **Do prices differ widely?** Yes; do a comparison shop since features will make a difference to the cost. If you're not going to use it much, there's no point in adding a big, unnecessary cost.

STEAM OVENS

Steam ovens have gained appeal because of their association with healthier cooking since they use moisture. Unless you're going to use it regularly, they're an unnecessary cost. "Some are tempted by wanting the newest and latest," says Wemlinger.

- ▶ **What are some negatives?** "Like induction cooking, it requires a learning curve," Wemlinger says. Steam ovens also don't brown or grill food.
- ▶ **What's the bottom line?** "Know your cooking and eating preferences," Wemlinger says.

REFRIGERATORS, FREEZERS, & SMALLER ASSISTANTS

Refrigeration has become a hot item with so many styles, colors, sizes, and smart features from which to choose. The selection is personal. But this is an expensive purchase that should last years. Some models are retro, others

This spread This kitchen designed by Lori Gilder, Interior Makeovers Inc., features the Miele 36-inch dual fuel range, 24-inch Combi-Steam oven, panel-ready Futura dishwasher, and a seamlessly integrated 36-inch refrigerator/freezer, complemented by the precision of Blanco sinks.

are industrial looking, and some are very spare and lean looking. Many can be all-in-one units with a freezer on the top, bottom, or side. Some models offer separate refrigerator and freezer "columns," if the homeowner has greater chilling/freezing needs, requires the extra space, wants to keep functions separate because of traffic flow, or has a bigger budget to indulge.

For older people or people with a disability, a side-by-side refrigerator and freezer (preferably 24 inches deep) with fully extendable shelves, can be easier to manage and requires less room to open.

Key considerations:

▶ **Do you want it freestanding or integrated?** A sleek built-in look is nice but is usually more of a commitment financially. The freestanding model is easier to take with you if or when you move. You need to be able to open and close the door and not have any obstructions, so be sure the cabinets are taken into consideration, Wemlinger says.

▶ **Do you need more interior space?** It's not just about the outside dimensions and what fits into the layout, but what's inside to store everything to avoid that second appliance in your garage or basement. Buyers should also look at the arrangement of bins, drawers, and temperature settings inside since freshness—and how long your lettuce stays crisp—matters more these days. Adjustable shelves are nice for those who have their own preference for storing food.

▶ **Is "instant" water or ice important, and is it best on the inside or outside?** To have either, you need a waterline nearby; adding one adds to the cost of installation, so ask a plumber in advance if this is a feature you desire.

▶ **Do you want it to stand out or fade into the room's backdrop?** Many models can have custom panels added to resemble the surrounding cabinetry.

NEO-1970S KITCHEN IN GREENWICH VILLAGE

In conversation with Eric, New York City, New York

In midcentury downtown New York City apartment buildings, a renovation of an estate apartment often means putting in a new kitchen. The kitchen in Eric's apartment in a 26-story, 1960s white-brick building is the largest he's had. The building was erected on the original site of the now defunct Wannamaker's department store. The apartment was owned for decades by a beloved Greenwich Village denizen. When first created, the kitchen was considered modern and stylish with its white laminated countertops, plaid contact paper, and Dutch blue accents. However, in 2021, when Eric bought the apartment, he insisted it be "taken down to the concrete."

For his kitchen, Eric wanted to create a contemporary riff on the '70s vibe to host intimate, all-out dinner parties for friends, colleagues, artists, and thinkers. An aspiring chef in his teens, and now a seasoned communications consultant to cultural institutions, Eric replicates and reinterprets this tradition five or six times a year.

Eric removed everything from the old kitchen, including cabinets, appliances, floors, and wiring. He also:

▶ retained the original footprint, but raised and widened the door frame to create an entryway more open to the dining area;

▶ removed the low-functioning, unsightly window exhaust fan;

▶ replaced the three-pane window with a new two-pane one, grounded with a white quartz sill, to create a visual focal point; and

▶ added a full suite of Bosch appliances, including a 30-inch counter-depth refrigerator for a streamlined look—the refrigerator is Wi-Fi enabled and connected to an app, so Eric can monitor it when he is away on one of his many trips.

To achieve the desired modern-meets-1970s vibe, Eric also added:

▶ custom deep olive-colored appliance fronts for the dishwasher and refrigerator to match the millwork, with matching chrome and Lucite cabinet hardware; and

▶ a backsplash wall of dimensional tile from Heath Ceramics, a supplier in the Bay Area.

Budget: Incorporated into the gut renovation of the entire apartment

Timeline: More than one year

Professionals involved: Eric worked with a local renovation firm, including an in-house designer, to make it work in practical terms, and an artist friend to realize the look and feel.

What sets it apart: The kitchen is a room equal to others in the apartment, with hardwood herringbone floors flowing. It's adjacent to the dining area—a welcoming space that is an important part of the home; not just a utility space.

Best feature: Heath Ceramics 3D-tile walls, from the Dimensional collection that was brought back to life in 2003 after lying dormant for 30 years in the Heath factory, according to the company website. The pattern adds to the 1970s ambiance with a modern-era twist.

Regrets: Further scrutiny of the first, second, and third set of contractor's measurements might have revealed additional possibilities and specific design solutions, such as storage for baking pans next to the stove, or a space above the refrigerator for a Danish modern 1960s red enamel salad bowl.

Lesson(s) learned: Be patient.

- ▶ **Do you want or need a refrigerator or freezer drawer?** When these debuted years ago, they were popular for those who had the space and funds. They could be placed in a different part of the room to keep traffic away from the main hub, at a height for kids to grab juice boxes or parents to store a bottle of wine, perhaps in a butler's pantry or family recreation room. There are also other options, such as icemakers. There are some models that come with locks and work off Wi-Fi. These can be the fun selections that improve home entertainment and everyday family life.
- ▶ **What are some of the smart features?** Some refrigerators now can provide an inventory of the food you have on hand, regulate temperature remotely, and diagnose issues to help a repair person solve any problems offsite.

DISHWASHERS

Many remember the old days when it was *de rigueur* to rinse items before placing them in the dishwasher. That's now passé, as dishwashers have become far better at removing everything, while also delicately washing fine crystal and good china—and quietly.

While the average width is 24 inches, smaller 18-inch models are available, which may be necessary for some homeowners with a small kitchen. Wemlinger cautions that even single homeowners who have tight kitchens might be wise to stay with 24 inches for those just-in-case scenarios. Another thing to think about, Feiden says, is whether it will fit with the surrounding cabinetry.

Key considerations:

- ▶ **Do you want adjustable racks inside with tines to separate items?** This offers peace of mind when you are mixing items, such as crystal and ceramic mugs, on the same row or rack.
- ▶ **Are there options regarding the loads and number of cycles?** Such options exist where you can choose between washing a small load compared to a large load. Many models offer this with cycles too, but you should decide if it really matters.
- ▶ **Does the idea of a dish drawer appeal?** These took off years ago and some like the idea of filling it up and then filling the other drawer.
- ▶ **Do you care about the noise level?** Insulation has been added to make many machines quieter, particularly important if you're going to be in the room while it's on or if you're in an open-plan layout where your dining- or living-room areas are within earshot.
- ▶ **Do you like to see the controls, or do you want them hidden?** Here again, there's a choice. Some let you know it's on and working by showing a red light on the floor when the machine runs.
- ▶ **Which models are the best models?** Many manufacturers offer different levels of quality with bells and whistles costing more; be sure you really need certain features if price is a factor. You will pay more for an interior fabricated from stainless steel versus plastic.

Above The large apron front fireclay sink adds durability and a visual break to the wood-wrapped kitchen. Custom cabinetry and paneling disguise appliances for a clean, cohesive design in this mountain home designed by Jennifer Robin, Jennifer Robin Interiors.

▶ **Will you need a second dishwasher for your lifestyle?** Some homeowners who observe certain religious occasions may want multiple appliances that serve the same purpose, as do those who entertain often and have lots of dishes to clean.

▶ **Do you want the machine to stand out or look integrated?** Some manufacturers allow stainless-steel panels or wood to be installed on the front to match cabinetry or a refrigerator.

▶ **What are smart features in dishwashers today?** A dishwasher may be able to shut off when dishes are clean rather than going through an entire cycle, which saves time and money. New options continue to emerge.

SINKS

Sinks come in lots of varieties, shapes, materials, and colors. When choosing one, keep in mind its length, width, and depth. An average sink measures up to 33 inches wide, Wemlinger says, and is eight to 10 inches deep, which is great for washing anything but especially that big lobster pot. "Be sure the sink is in proportion with the base cabinet it sits on," Wemlinger says.

Key considerations:

▶ **Do you want a big (farmhouse-style) sink or a double bowl?** Think about whether you like the idea of separating some items when hand washing or soaking.

▶ **What style do you like?** An apron front that has a bit of a farmhouse chic, or a deep undermount that may appear less visible? "Some favor

COASTAL HOME WITH LUXURY KITCHEN APPLIANCES & MORE

In conversation with Jeff, Carlsbad, California

Adjacent to a 1950s beach bungalow affectionately named "Surf Casa," owner Jeff sought to add an accessory dwelling unit (ADU). He wanted an upscale gourmet kitchen with top-notch appliances to be the centerpiece of the 700-square-foot home for cooking, dining, and entertaining in a small space.

He hired the design firm Interiors by Alison, owned by Alison Truelock and also located in Carlsbad, to build a structure that felt like it belonged with the original 1950s beachfront home but had a fresh, updated look. In taking this approach, Jeff could simultaneously enjoy his beachside property and rent the ADU to short-term visitors during peak months.

With the kitchen as the focal point, luxury appliances were installed, including a dual-fuel Wolf range; workstation sink with Newport Brass plumbing fixtures; microwave drawer; and a specialty LG refrigerator that makes craft ice for cocktails. Truelock sought to bring the outdoors indoors by adding skylights and a deck with large, sliding glass doors adjacent to the kitchen where the owners could enjoy sunset views. A local woodworker was commissioned to create an island from a large, live-edge, walnut slab, which became the center of the living areas. It also functions as both a prep area for cooking and a dining table, with stools for guests, and future entertaining opportunities.

Here are some of the features of the new space:

- Concrete quartz countertops on the perimeter, for easy maintenance
- A handmade backsplash (Avery Grande in Carrara Blanco marble from Stone Impressions) for a burst of pattern and color
- Oversized photography of the ocean, which flanks the wall opposite the sink to remind the owners of the beauty of the water
- Custom window treatments in a linen–cotton blend with decorative trim, which add softness and privacy to the large windows
- Engineered wide-plank white oak flooring that gives the room a soft, warm foundation
- Walls painted using Sherwin Williams Shoji White in a matte finish
- Deep navy custom cabinets in a satin finish; the trims and ceilings painted Pure White
- Brushed brass hardware that brings warmth to the space and maximizes storage

Budget: $55,000

Actual cost: $55,000

Timeline: Eight weeks

Professionals involved: Jeff hired the designer and contractor before engaging the architect who helped create the exterior vision. The interior designer worked with the contractor and homeowners to make creative suggestions and the general contractor scheduled framers, cabinet makers, plumbers, masons, electricians, painters, and flooring installers to make the space come to life.

Best feature: The large, live-edge, walnut island is an instant conversation piece. It elevates the room with its gorgeous shape and serves as a functional dining table as well.

What sets it apart: The owner, designer, and contractor worked together to create a transitional beach bungalow that contains a full kitchen with all the amenities of a luxury gourmet kitchen, including high-end appliances.

a drop-in sink because of the cost saving versus an undermount," Wemlinger says. Consider how it will look with the countertop, which can be the same or a different material.

▶ **Which material appeals?** Here, you can have your sink fade into the counter or stand out. Think whether you favor ceramic, stainless steel, enameled cast iron, enameled steel, quartz composite, granite composite, fireclay, or copper. One manufacturer, Elkay, makes its Quartz Luxe® models in vivid jewel colors and neutrals so you can match an appliance or build an entire color palette around a sink. Wemlinger likes the look of a copper sink, but says it requires maintenance, and adds, "You can't go wrong with stainless steel." You could also go the custom route with a concrete sink or really splurge with marble.

▶ **Are there specialty sinks?** Yes, trough sinks, which are long and narrow, are great for an extra place for people to dump ice or a pile of shrimp, for example. Many also like a small bar sink in a bar or butler's pantry.

▶ **Do you like the idea of accessories?** There's a host of options today that sit atop the sink, such as cutting boards, colanders, strainers, and caddies. They help keep the washing crew organized. Don't forget about the drain since there are choices here, too. You can go with a grid or pop-up drain, so check these out in person to see which one appeals to you.

SMALL APPLIANCES

There are many terrific new small appliances available these days, but, regrettably, most kitchens have limited counter space. Too many appliances on the counter can make a kitchen look cluttered and junky. Those who are lucky to have a walk-in pantry or butler's pantry may find it useful to store and use them there, but other homeowners must make a choice. Wemlinger suggests putting away anything used infrequently and then investing in the appliances you think you'll use most often, then leaving those on the countertop, on display, where they're easy to access.

A homeowner might consider adding an appliance garage to a corner of their kitchen or pantry to hide these various items when not in use. Among the small appliances—some of which are not very small—these are the most favored:

- Toaster oven or toaster
- Air fryer
- Blender
- Food processor
- Rice cooker
- Coffee and/or espresso machine
- Milk frother
- Ice-cream maker
- Standing and/or hand–held mixer
- Instant Pot
- Popcorn maker
- Wok
- Waffle maker
- Immersion blender
- Electric kettle or old-fashioned teapot
- Pizza oven for outdoors, and pizza stone for indoors
- Sous vide or vacuum sealing machine

CHAPTER 4

Twists & Turns in Tapware: Faucets, Handles, Hardware, & Hinges

Not too long ago, tapware was an afterthought, a bit player with utilitarian functions. Today, tapware has become more of a star. Its time has come as a kitchen focal point with style, statement, and greater purpose.

Why now? "Designers are always searching for the next cool item to go in a kitchen," says certified kitchen designer (CKD) Eric Goranson, host of podcast and radio show Around the House, interior designer, DIY expert, and construction educator in Portland, Oregon. Tapware still serves an important function, but today it can be a finishing touch to enhance the overall design or even be the main attraction in a kitchen plan. One great faucet at the main kitchen sink can add color or a sculptural look that's unexpected.

Tapware comes in a wide range of finishes, styles, shapes, and sizes and is everywhere in big-box stores, plumbing supply wholesale houses; kitchen design shops and showrooms; and even online. There are thousands of choices in a wide range of prices—from readymade and off the shelf to made-to-order pieces resembling sculptural works of art.

The different price levels reflect how the product is manufactured, its materials, and labor involved. And even at the lower to mid-range price points, there is a lot of bang for the buck. For instance, in mid-grade tapware, fashion designers such as Jason Wu (whose name became widespread when he designed an inaugural gown for former First Lady Michelle Obama) are putting their names on new collections.

WHAT'S TRENDING?

Mixing materials

It's 100 percent acceptable to mix materials—types and colors. Think modern bars and traditional knobs, mixing silver and gold, or adding a pop of color. Molly Switzer, associate kitchen and bathroom designer (AKBD), principal designer, and owner of Molly N Switzer Designs, LLC, in Portland, Oregon, says this is one of her favorite aspects of current trends. "The mix of finishes on a particular piece is helping to make it more of a standout and unique piece rather than just another brushed nickel fixture in the mix," she says.

Opposite A farmhouse-style sink fabricated in stainless steel continues as a countertop along the perimeter under the windows. Designed by Jeff Eakley, Bilotta Kitchen & Home, with Carol Kurth Architecture + Interiors and Legacy Construction

The variety of sizes and mix of knobs versus handles are used also to highlight a particular space that might be open to the kitchen, such as a beverage center or wine bar in a great room that might have a different finish or type but still works with the kitchen area.

It's also acceptable to use extremes such as traditional elements like cremone bolts on custom cabinetry or furniture pieces. And with all that's offered in tapware, some people prefer the extreme minimalistic approach of completely hidden hardware. "It's very much two very extreme design trends co–existing alongside one another," Switzer says. Like yin and yang.

Matching materials

Matching hardware on the refrigerator, oven, or even dishwasher to resemble the cabinetry color works well, too. "The same color for the hardware as for the cabinets, or a neutral one, will make them less visible, while the thin lines will emphasize the elegance of the kitchen," says Noah Taft, chief marketing officer of California Faucets in Huntington Beach, California.

Switzer contends that matching appliance pulls can be a challenge since they are not the same diameter as cabinet hardware. "It's important to be aware of the fact that if a line has an 18-inch appliance pull, [it] doesn't mean it should be mixed and/or matched on cabinetry."

Goranson addresses matching the knobs of the cabinetry to the faucet. "It can be tricky if you don't use the same manufacturer. Brushed brass in one brand might be a different color made by another brand. Be sure to have all [the] pieces in hand when you make choices. They have to work together, or

Above 210 Design House selected metal finishes to add a cohesive classic look, paired with sepia oak for the tall wall and burnished gold metallized high-gloss lacquer for the upper cabinets, back wall, and back side of the island.

Following pages The stars of this kitchen designed by Monica Lewis, CMKBD, MCR, UDCP, J.S. Brown & Co., include a Blanco undermount composite farm sink in Anthracite and a Delta® Cassidy™ pull-down spray faucet in Arctic Stainless.

you'll miss the mark." He adds, "I'm starting to see companies that are creating new finishes having to come up with their own cabinetry hardware to match."

Finishes

Homeowners right now are drawn to metallic finishes that reflect nature, such as iron ore, mica, and pyrite. These finishes bring warmth to the tapware, notes Garrison Hullinger, president of Studio Garrison, in Portland, Oregon. "I find the matte finishes in white or black to be big game changers. It's tapping the postmodern feel of Fantini Rubinetti and leaving the Lamborghini waxed finish for dull or matte. I'm also loving the knurling that is being moved from the levers/handles to other parts of the fixture, creating interest and appeal."

Because homeowners at nearly all price points want individualistic designs in their kitchens, Switzer is seeing some of the same. "It's the return of beautiful living finishes such as the unlacquered brasses, weathered bronzes, and waxed finishes." She explains that these allow the fixture to patina and change with use and exposure to different elements. "This creates a beautiful feeling of time-honored pieces."

Customization

Customizing tapware is also on the rise. In many kitchens, it's front and center. "In an island piece, we are installing showstopping work to draw attention to the very central workhorse of a space. Depending on the style of the home and preferences by clients, we see very sleek and easy-to-clean pieces, as well as intricate and detailed fixtures that look as if instructions for use should be tagged alongside it for any new user," says Switzer.

Switzer says styles that are "hot" right now, especially in luxury projects, include modern/contemporary and detailed, as well as traditional, and a lot of transitional that's on entry and mid-range work being done. "It bridges several styles and is easy to work with," she says.

FAUCETS: OFF THE SHELF TO BESPOKE

Faucets now come in an array of styles including classic, modern, transitional, art deco, and steampunk, for starters. Some faucets are old-school polished chrome with handles that you twist; some you tap to turn on. They can come voice-activated with eco-friendly personal settings where you can control water activation, temperature, and amounts without lifting a finger. Then there are the modular sinks and faucets, all in one unit, that save space. Faucets come in single-hole, two-hole, three-hole, and bridge construction with an array of handles, levers, wheels, and height options. Taft adds that there is serious interest today in faucets beyond polished chrome and brushed nickel; now, interest lies in matte black; brass tones; more exotic finishes; and graphite (dark gray charcoal). "Overall, faucets have become more stately—bigger, more arching, look professional or commercial," Taft says. His company works in solid brass to create over 25 finishes.

Kymberly Glazer, director of marketing and sales at Decorative Plumbing + Hardware Association, based in Bethesda, Maryland, says she is seeing many more interesting and mixed finishes in faucets, as well as commercial-inspired designs scaled for a residential kitchen. "I would say that 90-plus percent of the kitchen faucet designs are single-hole and pull-down. I'm not yet seeing many new bridge faucet designs or three-holes," Glazer adds.

"A kitchen faucet is the most used faucet in the home," says Armando Gonzales, sales consultant at Ferguson Bath, Kitchen & Lighting Gallery, New York City, New York. "Sixty percent of people buying faucets still go with standard polished chrome or polished or matte nickel, and an off-the-shelf item that doesn't require production time. To them, a faucet is a faucet, while more are starting to see it as integral to the overall design. They come in with samples of countertops, paint colors, fabrics, floors, and backsplashes."

Colors, finishes, & functions

Here are the most popular kitchen faucet colors, finishes, and functions, according to the *2023 Design Trends* report by the NKBA:

- ▶ **Colors:** Stainless steel, black, and nickel
- ▶ **Finishes:** Brushed, matte, satin, polished, natural, and antique
- ▶ **Functions (most to least popular):** Lever, touch/tap, motion control, voice activated, cross handles/dual handle, and foot pedal control

Technology

Technology at its best makes life easier. According to the NKBA report, "Homeowners are adopting technology at a faster pace, specifically when it enables more individualized customization in the kitchen (and bath)."

Here are some of the ways homeowners are using technology in tapware, according to the same report:

- ▶ To create a personalized environment, using app/voice controls for lighting, water, and floor temperatures, as well as humidity monitoring
- ▶ To have touchless faucets, app-controlled appliances, whole house systems
- ▶ To conserve water

Above (left to right) A fireclay farmhouse sink by Herbeau sits on the perimeter of a country-style kitchen with a classic gooseneck faucet and side sprayer in a chrome finish; A sculptural faucet by Waterstone and its matching filtered faucet, both in antique pewter, arc over double undermount sinks from Franke; The clean-lined, stainless-steel single-bowl undermount sink by Franke is enhanced by single-hole faucets. Three separate kitchens designed by Bilotta Kitchen & Home

Opposite The double-bowl white porcelain farmhouse sink works in conjunction with the Rohl nickel gooseneck single-lever faucet and sprayer, and a garbage disposal button inset in the countertop slab. Kitchen designed by Susan Brunstrum, Studio Brunstrum

Goranson, who is also a tech speaker for the National Association of Home Builders (NAHB), thinks tech is important. "But I don't like dumb technology. For example, I don't need my faucet to tell me what the weather is going to be tomorrow, but if it measures a cup of water without my having to grab a measuring cup, fabulous," he says. Switzer sees more successful technologies integrated into tapware with touch or touch-free fixtures. "This strong uptick in client interest comes directly from the impact of the pandemic, bringing a huge push for better performing, hands-free, residential fixture options." Gonzales says in terms of high tech in faucets, he mostly sees sales of filtered hot, cold, and sparkling water dispensers coming out of the same faucet in a range of styles.

Buying a quality faucet

Switzer estimates that for a quality faucet in a kitchen, a homeowner should expect to spend $700 plus. The more decorative ones are obviously going to be well over the $1,500 mark, but a quality piece is going to get used constantly so it needs to hold up. The warranty will reflect this, as well as the materials used. "I tell clients to pick up a faucet box. If it doesn't surprise you how hefty it is, it's not a quality piece. Brass construction is key, and brass is not lightweight," she says.

On the other hand, Goranson says you can pay from under $100 and up to $12,000 for a customized faucet. Gonzales advises not cutting corners. "Purchase one that is well made even if it costs a bit more. You're not just buying a faucet for function but are purchasing a certain element that adds cachet and quality to your design," he says.

Here are some questions to ask when searching for your own faucet:
► How is the faucet made/manufactured?
► What is it made of?
► Is the coating on the outside durable and/or will it tarnish? Just because it's made of copper inside, it needs to have a baked-on finish. And now those finishes come in many colors.
► What is the "life expectancy" of the faucet? Plastic insides may last five to 20 years, but if a faucet is entirely metal, stainless steel, or expensive bronze, it could be around longer than the owner.
► Does it come with a warranty or any guarantees?

HARDWARE: THE KITCHEN'S JEWELRY

Hardware, handles, and hinges are the kitchen equivalent of bling in the same way that jewelry adds pizzazz or a touch of class to an outfit. Most hardware comes in finishes similar to faucets in various shapes, sizes, and styles.

Before selecting any hardware, Switzer is adamant about having the door style and sizes confirmed. "There is the scenario that you design around the hardware, but more often it is easier to start with your finished cabinet design than work on hardware in order to keep client stress levels low," she says.

Do you need to use a certain type of hardware or handle/knob with a certain style cabinet? A certain color? According to Switzer, finishes or colors really depend on the overall design style. "More often a client wants the hardware to be a bit of jewelry in the space, so we see a higher contrast to the cabinet coloring. But in the sleek minimalistic designs, we see thinner profiles and finishes that do not stand off the cabinetry as boldly."

Hullinger loves the sleek lines of a finger pull. "I also like using a complementary style of hardware pulls/knobs with the interior door sets of the home. I think using different types of hardware within a space is appropriate based on the programming of the space," he says.

Size

Does a certain size handle have to go on a certain size cabinet or drawer? Sizing in a kitchen is influenced by backsplashes and windowsills. "A good rule to follow is to size the pull to one-third the width of the cabinet or drawer front. Appliance pulls should be a minimum of 20 inches in length," Hullinger says. For large drawers, Switzer says she aims for a one-third-to-half-an-inch rule. In all scenarios, she fits client hand sizing directly with the particular handles in question to ensure they are both comfortable and proportional to a client's particular hand size. "Nobody wants a situation where a client's hand simply cannot fit within the space provided."

Is there ever a need for two handles on a drawer? Switzer says, "There are exactly zero scenarios in which putting two handles on a wide drawer should be acceptable. It will cause uneven movement to the cabinet and eventually cause the slides to fail."

Placement

As a fan of finger pulls, Hullinger likes them to be centered on drawers and placed on the lower corner of the upper cabinets and upper corner of the lower cabinets. Placing the finger pulls on cabinet doors over an exhaust fan or the top row of drawers on a deeper overhang of counter might require a deeper finger pull.

Switzer tries to center her knobs on the stile and rail of a cabinet door corner. She starts her vertical handles on a cabinet the same way unless it's being used as a pantry or a taller piece, which requires centralized placement for ease of use. "When it comes to a drawer face, it depends on the style of the drawer front, and the sheer size of the drawers. The main thought on this is in the scenario of a handle, a small top drawer will often be too small to place a handle in the central part of the door face without scraping knuckles on a door with a recessed door face," Switzer says.

She adds that too often a designer might install a handle on the top rail of a drawer to avoid this issue entirely. "Slab door faces make it very easy to mount handles on the center of the face without issue. Based on the size and style of the door, this often works well," Switzer explains. "We put handles near the top in large, deep, pull-out drawers such as garbage/recycle receptacles and mount the handle parallel to the floor for ease of ergonomic opening," she says.

Price range

For knobs, handles, and pulls, Switzer says to "expect to pay five to ten dollars each for basic hardware." Most pieces over six inches long will be over $15; then 12 inches or more will be $25 to $40. Anything longer can cost over $50.

HINGES

Hinges, too, are being noticed and now come in nickel, chrome, matte black, bronze with copper highlights, oil-brushed bronze, and more to match the plethora of hardware choices. Some types include full overset, inlay, self-closing overlay, overlay concealed, spring closing inset hinge, and flush mount.

Switzer, Hullinger, and Goranson prefer a soft-close, so it doesn't bang the cabinet and leave marks. "The type is based on the cabinet box style," says Hullinger. Goranson, who likes the screws inside, says hinges should be as small as possible—a slim rectangle and compact so they stay out of the way. He adds that since hinges usually come with new cabinets, they do not incur an extra cost and have a lifetime warranty.

When it comes to door hinges and slides, Switzer uses soft-close from ball bearing to concealed, to spring loaded. It depends on the function, weight, and style of the door. She'll match door hinges to hardware finish, but when there's a split finish, where the exterior may be satin nickel, but the interior finish might be polished brass, she'll coordinate the finish with the hinges at the same time.

ACCESSORIES

It's the little things that count. Today, customers want a full suite of products. This includes main water fixtures, disposal buttons, air gaps, soap dispensers, hot/cold and filtered taps, pot fillers, and bar faucets that all coordinate within a single line so there's no need to go to another unless they want to mix and match for different reasons.

Switzer warns that pulling all accessories together from different brands and thinking they're "close enough" can be a problem. "Brands are finally hearing our designer cries for this, and I believe they are seeing the benefits of larger sales because of it," Switzer says.

If your head is reeling from all the choices, comfort yourself with this thought: tapware today can give a new twist to your kitchen design that can either be a minimalistic whisper, make a subtle statement, or be a shout out that inspires the entire kitchen design and becomes its star.

INDUSTRIAL CUSTOM FAUCET AS THE CENTERPIECE OF A GALLEY KITCHEN

In conversation with Eric and Julie, Portland, Oregon

After Eric and his wife, Julie, bought their 1970s angled contemporary two-story home in November 2019, Eric leapt at the chance to redo the kitchen. After all, he's a pro—a certified kitchen designer, interior designer; DIY expert; construction educator; and host of *Around the House* show on radio and TV.

However, there was a twist. For a decade, Eric had his eye on a large, expensive, "punk looking" Waterstone Endeavor Wheel Faucet with lever sprayer, which is bronze, and finished in matte black and brushed gold. "To me, it was like a beautiful, handcrafted piece of art." In fact, it made a such a statement that he designed his entire kitchen around it after purchasing it for $9,000, far more than most faucets.

When the couple bought the house, the kitchen had never been updated and had a little laundry area, tiny countertops, and a peninsula. "We kept the same footprint, but we extended it out as far as we could by removing the pantry and laundry area," Eric says. The laundry area now houses the refrigerator. "We also removed the five-foot, walled-in pantry that made space for the 48-inch dual fuel range," he says. These changes more than doubled the countertop space and storage.

All cabinetry is custom and done in a white matte finish with a slab door. The countertops are Dupont Corian® Endura High Performance Porcelain. Cabinet T-Bar hardware is Buster + Punch—solid metal, characterized by the diamond-cut, cross knurl pattern in brass. Appliances are ZLINE except for the LG refrigerator (ZLINE's refrigerator was not in production at the time). They kept the original white oak floors.

Eric's passion for the faucet is similar perhaps to why men are so driven to care about cars. It combines "wow" factor with function. "The faucet is the one thing people walk over to it and ask, 'What is this?' and they have to touch it and try it," he says. Mission accomplished.

Just a few feet off the kitchen is their 1970s black leather and walnut raised bar with four stools that they "grabbed out of an estate sale." The hardware, outlet covers, switches, and knobs match the kitchen ones with the same knurled design.

"We are happy with the way it turned out. I call it my pandemic kitchen. My wife and I both love to cook, and we can cook together comfortably in this space. And it's only 20 feet from our outdoor kitchen," Eric adds.

Budget: They stayed on budget. Eric estimates that the kitchen today would cost about $125,000 to assemble.

Professionals involved: Eric did all the work himself, except he had the countertops fabricated.

Timeline: Six months.

Biggest challenge: The faucet weighs 35 pounds; "that's how much brass it has in it—so I had to design a countertop structure that could take the weight of the faucet," Eric says.

Regrets: "I wish I could have made the space bigger without doing an addition, moving staircases, or taking on a larger project," Eric says.

Lesson(s) learned: "Most of what I did in our kitchen I have done hundreds of times. I did learn, however, that materials were hard to come by, and I had to be patient with lead times," Eric says.

CHAPTER 5

Islands: Centerpieces of Today's Kitchens

Islands have been around for decades, long ago replacing peninsulas as an extra workspace, but they haven't always been the main attraction. Years ago, it was a big, six-burner range or built-in, stainless-steel refrigerator with a recognizable brand name that stole the show. Even a wine refrigerator, apron sink, or pot filler achieved the same effect in different ways. Each of these items can set one kitchen apart from another, both aesthetically and functionally. However, more recently, islands have moved up on homebuyers' wish lists because they accommodate so many functions. New York City-based designer Rozit Arditi, principal and founder of Arditi Design, likes to include an island where there's need for multiple tasks in one central spot—from gathering for breakfast or lunch, to catering for cocktail hour when entertaining. It can also be the main conversation area while cooking or cleaning up. If there is still a competition for star billing, most experts believe the winner, hands down, is an island.

Today, islands are constructed bigger than ever before—kitchens are larger now and often part of an open-plan layout. Larger islands can also fit more seating, inspire large-scale light choices, or allow for several pendant lights above to match the dimensions. An island's size can accommodate appliances and show off great creativity.

An island must work in sync with the room's other features and homeowners' needs to be successful. The following key factors should influence its functionality and aesthetics.

SIZE

The size of an island should be based in part on the room's dimensions so it's proportional to the entire space, and can accommodate all needs—eating, storage, cooking, mixing drinks, serving, and socializing. Jodi Swartz thinks the minimum size should be 36 by 42 inches. She doesn't like to go larger than one stone slab for the top that measures 60 by 120 inches, or five by 10 feet, to avoid seams. Suzan Wemlinger agrees for another, more practical reason: "It's harder to reach the center of a very large island to clean it well."

If the room isn't large, an alternative may be a peninsula—once a very popular (and still viable) solution, says designer Fabrice Garson of Bilotta Kitchen & Home in the New York area.

Opposite Jean Liu Design combines both form and function with a versatile marble island that juxtaposes well against the white oak wood floor.

Following pages This colorful kitchen designed by Morgante Wilson Architects features an island inspired by the artwork of Piet Mondrian, which boasts custom steel side panels in a geometric pattern, primary blue cabinets, and a white quartzite top.

PLACEMENT

Where the island fits best in the layout will affect its size. It shouldn't be in the way of foot-traffic paths to other rooms or block access to an appliance or pantry. The amount of space between the island and perimeter countertops and cabinetry is another consideration. Many professionals advise a distance of 42 to 48 inches between a countertop and island, so both surfaces can be reached with just a step or two. The NKBA recommends 42 inches minimum, as this measurement also permits two people to pass and a dishwasher or oven to have its door open with room to safely walk by.

MAIN FUNCTIONS

Most islands now have multiple purposes: eating, storage, food preparation, serving, cleaning, and schoolwork. Some islands have more than one level for separate functions, such as mixing drinks at a small bar sink on an upper level—higher than the usual 36-inch-high island and counter height—and comfortably rolling out pastry on a lower level—usually 30 to 33 inches high.

Appliances can also be built into an island. When Bilotta Kitchen & Home designers initially meet with a client, they talk about their lifestyle, preferences, and dream space and design around that, including the island. Garson says, "Some like to have a secondary prep sink so while cutting veggies, they have an abundance of space. Some want a second dishwasher. Some also want their range or cooktop with seating across from the island, so they can cook and engage with people at the same time."

Super large kitchens are increasingly designed with two islands, so one isn't too large, out of scale or unwieldy to get around. Functions can be divided between the islands. Garson has designed one island solely for sitting/gathering, homework, and eating, and the other island has a sink and some appliances to serve as a "real workstation."

SEATING

For comfortable seating, many suggest the standard 35.75 to 36-inch counter height rather than a higher 42-inch bar height. Keep in mind that appliances installed in an island may affect its height, since standard dishwasher height is no more than 34.25 inches. For an ADA (Americans with Disabilities Act) application, which requires a reduced height, any undercounter appliances would need to be specified accordingly.

CABINET CONSTRUCTION

For storage—whether on the island or an adjacent perimeter—many pros recommend drawers since they offer only one motion to open, pull out, and put back what's needed. Heights within should vary to fit what's stored, which can mean deep for large pots or small appliances that are stored away. Some people favor open shelves to store cookbooks and oft-used measuring cups, and to display utensils and collectibles.

This spread A large Calacatta marble island accentuated by polished stainless-steel straps and details serves as a center for activity in this kitchen designed by Nancy J. Ruddy and Ximena Rodriguez, CetraRuddy, with cabinetry designed by Christopher Peacock.

COUNTERTOP MATERIALS

Swartz's first rule of thumb is that homeowners understand that no material is 100 percent indestructible. That means they should not take anything hot off a range or from an oven and place it directly on any island surface (or perimeter countertop) but instead rest it atop a trivet or other heatproof surface. What's popular now, according to Garson, are maintenance-free engineered surfaces that look good and can be used without too much worry about damage from heat, spills of acid or wine, and scratches from cutting. Sometimes homeowners integrate a butcherblock or live-edge section within a top or extend that material to warm up the island's look. Some clients like a marble section for rolling out pastry. Other features include polished, stainless-steel straps around edges of Calacatta marble and brushed stainless-steel combinations.

A new stone choice for islands is Dekton, an ultra-compact material made up of over 20 minerals and without any resins. Dekton is heat and stain resistant. It comes in different textures, from leather to honed and matte to glossy, and can range in appearance from the look of natural quartzite to a metallic finish. "It's a stunning material that can also be installed in outdoor kitchens as it won't fade or soften in the sun," says Sandya Dandamudi, president of Chicago-based GI Stone. "Like porcelain, it is not a true body, so the edge will not reflect the print on the top of the countertop. However, a mitered edge or bevel back edge is one way to finish the edges to blend well with the top. Or the edge can be cut and polished as some people like the dual tonality."

While Dekton is a bit more expensive to cut and fabricate, its raw material cost ranges from $20 to $40 per square foot. Comparably, the raw material cost of quartzite, granite, or marble can vary widely, from $8 per square foot all the way to $200 per square foot. "Overall, Dekton can be a cost-effective choice considering what it delivers," she says. It is important to remember that prices vary in different markets for various reasons, so always check.

Previous pages Landry Design Group uses dual islands topped in Polar White quartzite to serve different purposes—one features a large double faucet sink for food prep, and the second serves as a breakfast bar and buffet, with integrated Sub-Zero refrigerator drawers.

Above The Turett Collaborative uses gray glass sustainable cabinets and a stone-top island inspired by Valcucine's Italian design collections.

Opposite A mix of materials and finishes makes this blue gloss island pop against the walnut butcher block above, contrasting with the quartzite counters and handmade ceramic tile backsplash. Designed by Kaufman Segal Design

Following pages This over-scaled island with a reclaimed wood surface designed by Kaufman Segal Design creates the perfect centerpiece and place to gather and entertain.

Opposite In a compact kitchen designed by Lori Gilder, Interior Makeovers Inc., and Rebecca Reynolds Design, the island helps elevate efficiency and style with its 24-by-24-inch mobile design on lockable casters.

Above A single-height island, measuring 42 by 96 inches, offers plenty of room for meal prep in a kitchen designed by Meredith Young, CKD, J.S. Brown & Co. Natural walnut accents tie in the stained woodwork of the adjacent rooms, with full overlay cabinetry painted in Benjamin Moore's Carolina Gull. The Ivybridge™ quartz countertop by Cambria® has hints of teal and gold to meld the colors of the island and finishes of the plumbing and light fixtures.

PERMANENT OR MOVABLE

Some designers and homeowners include a table or other piece of furniture for a less utilitarian look or a trolley atop wheels or casters, so the island, usually not very large, can move about the room or even into adjoining areas. "It makes the space flexible and accommodating," Swartz says. The downside of a table as the island is it becomes less practical since it usually won't have storage, be at the best height for most tasks, or have electric outlets.

EXTRAS

As islands have become workhorses, they need more outlets to accommodate all the appliances that may be used on them, and they should be located within easy reach, says Ximena Rodriguez, principal and director of interior design at CetraRuddy, an architecture and interior design firm based in New York City, New York. A drawer in an island can become a good place to set up a charging station—what's referred to as a "docking drawer"—for cell phones, tablets, and even computers and keep them accessible but out of sight or at risk of misplacement. Homeowners can also tuck into the island a dog-bowl station for food and water, an additional chopping block on wheels, or a fold-out table.

COLORS, PATTERNS, & TEXTURES

White kitchens still rank No. 1 in popularity but introducing another color or material in the island when there's lots of white on perimeter countertops and cabinets can help differentiate the island and add punch to a room. Swartz finds that some color will make the island look more custom. But she offers some caveats. "I think scale is important. If a kitchen is on the smaller side, and the perimeter isn't long, I believe that keeping the same stone on an island makes the space look bigger," she says. And another: "If the island is meant to be utilitarian, I think a different counter or cabinet looks great," she says. "If it is meant to make the 'statement' in the room, I believe it can be completely different. But it depends on how many 'pink flamingoes' or 'focal points' (might) work. In larger spaces, you can change it up." Garson finds that more of his clients now want a different material or color for the island than what they use around the perimeter. Dandamudi also observes that the mix-and-match look is exploding. "Several of our clients select quartz counters for the perimeter, which includes around the sink and cooktop, and opt for an exotic natural stone for the island and backsplashes. This is a great way to combine practical needs and aesthetic tastes," she says.

Keep in mind the possible long-term consequences for mixing and matching. "Short of white or cream—what isn't trendy?" Swartz asks. "Cabinets are fashion. Some elements go out of style every 10 to 15 years. People should choose wisely and best match the feel of their home's architecture," she suggests.

HOW THE WORK TRIANGLE WORKS WITH AN ISLAND

The work triangle, a concept formulated by NKBA, states that a cook should be able to easily reach the cooking, cleaning, and food storage areas, which occupy the points on a triangle. There should also be enough space between those areas to eliminate crowding. As kitchens have gotten bigger, some have gained a second or even third work triangle, one of which may be totally within the island or just one of its legs that works in conjunction with other areas of the room.

The architects and designers at CetraRuddy like to incorporate a sink in an island so that it forms a triangle with the oven and the refrigerator on the perimeter and simplifies movement between these three critical places.

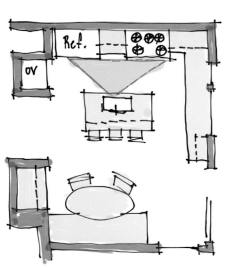

Previous pages Bilotta Kitchen & Home uses a stone top of a deep eggplant-colored island and a bundle of branches to support an organic island perch fashioned from a 48-inch live-edge slice of a twin maple. Architecture by Clark Neuringer, Clark Neuringer Architects

Below Ana Williamson, Ana Williamson Architect, Menlo Park, California, sketches a kitchen work triangle, known as "the golden triangle" in kitchen parlance, which depicts three main work areas—the sink/counter, refrigerator, and the range—and allows for ease of daily kitchen tasks.

THE ISLAND THAT STOLE THE SHOW

In conversation with Marty and Peggy, Sea Cliff, Long Island, New York

The 1927 bungalow-style home near the water has been a family keepsake for more than 50 years, first rented by Marty's sister as a summer getaway from her New York City apartment and then by Marty and wife Peggy, between 1983 and 1990. They too wanted an escape from Manhattan, but then later purchased it as their full-time residence.

Marty and Peggy were determined to transform the small kitchen into one that looked better and was more functional. Among the couple's first changes was opening the kitchen to the adjacent dining room by removing a wall, adding a skylight and two big windows in the combined space, and installing sliding glass doors on a large deck. They renovated but their choices of what was stylish back then—brown cabinets and black granite countertops—hardly looked stylish and inviting after a few years.

Marty and Peggy eventually knew they wanted a bright white kitchen with a larger island and more storage. They retained the room's Mexican tiled floor since it continued throughout the first level. They decided to keep the existing stainless-steel appliances and white, farm-style sink because they all worked well and still looked good.

They decided on a very white quartzite top in Iceberg, a stone from Brazil that has both crystalline and water qualities, which sparkles in the light. Also on their list were stools and stainless-steel pulls and knobs to personalize the room.

Early on, the contractor pointed out the home's original chimney, encased in sheetrock that was being removed. "We knew there was a chimney, but didn't know how attractive it might be," Marty says. It abuts the refrigerator on a short side wall and adds valuable charm and patina. Marty and Peggy chose a high-end, Shaker-style, white-painted cabinet, and added a few glass fronts to make the room seem lighter. They doubled the size of the existing island to be 40 by 84 inches—as large as it could be while still permitting easy movement around all four sides. They also added some shallow cabinet shelves on the dining-room side, where they stash kitchen supplies. New backsplashes are lined with two-by-six-inch white, subway-style tiles.

The relatively simple transformation has given them joy indoors and outdoors with the deck gaining a hot tub and more of Marty's sunflowers in big planters. A year or so after the work was completed, they added a new range and refrigerator.

Budget: $50,000

Actual cost: $50,000

Timeline: Four months

Professionals involved: A contractor who was a carpenter, skilled in installing choices in an older home with angles and uneven floors or walls, and an architect to stamp drawings for approval.

What sets it apart: Due to a prior remodeling, there is a rich amount of light that enters the kitchen. The old chimney, which isn't uniformly perfect but reveals the house's age, as well as the tiled floors, are both nice touches when everything else is brand spanking new.

Regrets: Choosing quartzite, because it is easily etched and stained and has required frequent sealing and cleaning. Also, Marty says, "Sometimes, I wish I had put a small sink in the island but that would have eliminated some of the storage, so we make do."

Lesson(s) learned: Stay at home to observe progress and catch potential problems. If something bothers you, speak up. Additionally, Marty recommends to "go the extra yard to achieve quality."

CHAPTER 6

Think (in) Color

Amy Wax, winner of the HUE Award from paint manufacturer Benjamin Moore, is the creator of the award-winning Color911 app, Color911.com or 1-877-Color911. She is former President of the National Association of Color Consultants / North America and author of the best-selling *Can't Fail Color Schemes: Kitchens and Baths*. Her website is AmyWax.com.

Color is the secret ingredient that transforms a kitchen and completes the picture. When choosing colors—for walls, backsplashes, appliances, floors, ceilings, and countertops—there is a dizzying array of choices, but all components must be in color harmony for the room to have the right *joie de vivre*. There is no single allegiance, which can cause a homeowner's head to reel. Even when it comes to white, there are hundreds of options—some with a hint of yellow, pink, blue, or other hues.

To start, ask yourself: Do you want colors that evoke a childhood memory or ones that are more recent? Perhaps you admired a color in someone's home or fell in love with one during a hotel stay. Another option is to go with a palette that ties in with the style and mood of the rest of your home, whether the kitchen is open or closed. Are your colors of choice bright or muted? Mellow or loud? Dark or light? Playful pinks and yellows? Shades of white and gray can be soulful and calming.

Green is a recent kitchen color trend. It implies freshness, health, balance, and natural goodness—all of which were sought during the Covid pandemic. Blues, particularly soft blue-gray and blue-green, are easygoing and very appealing to use for rooms where you spend a lot of time. If you add a rich navy or midnight blue, it has the elegance of saturated charcoal or black, with a friendlier vibe and a bit more personality. Add brushed gold hardware to any color cabinetry and you're upping your game to make a room as formal and elegant as any room in the house!

Amy Wax, color expert and author, works on both exteriors and interiors of homes and always considers architecture. She offers some pointers on how to choose the right color palette.

▶ **With today's trends, what is the best way to achieve balance in choosing color for a kitchen?**
The best way is to clearly define the ambiance and vibe that you want to express. Is your goal to create a space that is light and airy? Maintain that sense of style with everything you choose, whether it be the cabinets, backsplash, or floor material.
If you are looking to create more of a library feel in the room, keep that in mind when you are choosing the type of woods and textures.

Opposite "Blue is a timeless choice that pairs well with classic kitchen elements, such as stainless-steel appliances and brass hardware," says Kristi Will, Kristi Will Interior Design, Half Moon Bay, California. She uses a high gloss lacquer finish to create a sleek, modern aesthetic.

Every element contributes to the sense of balance and every element has a color. Keeping all colors consistent with the mood you want to create keeps your new design in balance. This is possibly one of the most important aspects of your design.

▶ **White kitchens remain the No. 1 choice, yet there are many shades of white paint. How do you choose shade and finish?**
Whites range from glowing and bright to warm and inviting. What makes the white kitchen so appealing—going from a trend to a gold standard—is cleanliness, the best feel-good vibe you could ask for in the room of food preparation and family gatherings.

If you are choosing white for your kitchen, take a close look at the rooms next to your kitchen. Would a bright white flow from the adjacent rooms into the kitchen or would a warmer color palette feel more appropriate? As a rule, if white is the primary color of cabinetry, a brighter white looks newer and fresher but select one that is not sterile. A warmer white is relaxed and easier on the eyes. Here I suggest a richer shade of white. Try to select one that's not too creamy or yellow, colors that create a completely different look. It is no longer a white kitchen. Another direction to go in is to choose a very, very pale gray. This creates a more contemporary atmosphere and allows for whiter elements like your backsplash and countertops to really shine.

In terms of finishes, it's important the white you select is completely washable. A low luster or pearl finish offers a subtle and softer shine on your cabinets, and it will still be washable. A higher shine, like a semi-gloss, is a harder finish. It will take more wear and tear and have a more polished appearance.

▶ **How do you choose among the different whites that work well together for cabinetry, countertops, backsplashes?**
In choosing the whites for your kitchen, it's extremely important to see them in the same light in which they will appear in your home. Whether paint, stone, or wood colors, all elements should be selected in residential lighting versus showroom lighting. Imagine a white marble backsplash or countertop. It's not just white. Often there is more gray running through the stone than white. It is important to see both the countertop and cabinetry in the same light to discern the subtle tones in your whites so that you can match the colors exactly. When the colors have the same undertones, whether gray or off-white, it makes for a much better design as the colors are in harmony.

▶ **Are there other colors that hold up in a kitchen?**
Yes. I believe that two families of colors will hold up longer and will stand the test of time. The first are those in the neutral family such as warm grays, a taupe, or very pale gray along with complementary natural colors. They can be mixed with almost any color accent if you choose to brighten up the room. This gives you the opportunity to personalize your space.

Opposite Eddie Maestri, AIA, Maestri Studio, employs multiple colors in this kitchen: green cabinets on the perimeter, black La Cornue range, oak island with a walnut stain, crisp white quartzite countertops, and a multicolored stained-glass window original to the home.

Above Alison Truelock, Interiors by Alison, uses lively navy blue in this tiny kitchen to play off the patterned tile and warm white walls. Architecture by Marcela & Logan Architects; Build by Jeremy Parsons, Oregon Trail Remodeling

Following pages A mosaic backsplash adds visual interest to this kitchen by Jeffrey Neve, Jeffrey Neve Interior Design, San Francisco Bay Area, California. The painted center island is the perfect counterpoint to the walnut cabinetry. The leather counter stools introduce another shade of blue.

The second family of colors that I believe will hold up over time are dustier colors—slate blues, softer golds, and grays with a hint of color like a gray-blue or a muted gray-green. These create a softer impression. They will flow from any style in the rest of your home and have a more casual feel. If you think some of these colors are old fashioned, it's quite the opposite. These colors never get old and maintain their sense of honesty and true charm, and create a more relaxing, stress-free atmosphere. This is a concept we can live with for a very long time.

► **If you choose a neutral like gray or white, how can you add a punch of color—and where?**
If you have white cabinetry in the kitchen, the beauty of this choice is that, by adding color, you can make a personal statement in your kitchen. One choice is to keep it simple and clean. Here, less is more without bright, colorful accent colors so that the colors in the room are created by other elements in the space.

If you choose to add color, there are three levels. The first is to paint the room. Imagine a kitchen with white cabinetry and light terracotta walls. You have made a softer statement, and you can bring in more color in soft furnishings: towels, rugs, chair cushions, and artwork. The beauty of this approach is that you can change out any or all of those colorful elements in an afternoon and shift the look of the whole room.

A second way of adding color into a white kitchen is to add a colorful tile backsplash. This can be the focal point in the room. Imagine a beautiful, polished glass tile backsplash with aquatic teal-blues, navy, and cool grays. It's the perfect accent to a white kitchen, and a beautiful statement in a colorless room. In choosing the style of backsplash, you have a wide variety of options including patterned mosaics, reflective mirror finishes, colored glass, polished stone, or even iridescent tile colors. The world is your oyster, and it's your opportunity to choose colors that make the whole room sing.

Finally, an easy and fun way of incorporating pops of color in your kitchen is to add appliances and functioning pieces that are colorful and make a bolder statement. Imagine a kitchen with a red mixer with chrome detailing, red teapot on the stove, and red hand towels. You also have the choice of adding colorful glassware in glass-doored cabinets. There are many companies that now offer colorful appliances and dishes. It's a fun way to add both color and spirit.

Opposite This kitchen was designed by Paula Winter, Paula Winter Design, to welcome as much light and brightness as possible. Architecture by Richard Becker, AIA, Becker Architects

Above Cooking with the featured BlueStar® range in red-brown paint is now easy after an island's shape was angled to create an aisle for hardworking prep and dining space, while cleanup is located on the other side of this "red hot" kitchen designed by Jodi Swartz, KitchenVisions, and general contractor Dishington Construction/Jensen Hus.

▶ **Are there any tricks to transforming a space using color—make it seem more intimate, larger or wider?**

There are many rooms where the color reflects a mood. Because there are many areas in your kitchen that carry a lot of color, I suggest thinking of them individually in regard to how they affect the visual size of the space. For example, if your cabinets are bright and the room feels open, a darker wall color will make the cabinets feel brighter and not darken the space or make it feel smaller. If you only have lower cabinets, then a darker wall color will darken the room, making it feel smaller and cozier. Light walls will support the feeling of the room being open and airy.

My suggestion is to look at the color that is at eye level or the most prominent, and let that color determine the size of your room. If you love a darker, more dramatic space, then a rich slate blue wall color will make the room feel more intimate and that might be just the feel you are seeking.

If what is at eye level is bright white or light wood cabinets, then the color of the wall will not really affect the size of the room. It's the color of the cabinets that will mark the visual size of the room. The wall color simply supports it. What seems to matter most is the color of your cabinets and the aesthetic you are trying to accomplish.

This spread Jennifer Robin, Jennifer Robin Interiors, added some drama to this neutral-colored space with the large-scale chandelier contrasting against the oak-paneled wall. The palette stays relatively quiet so that the surrounding views can take center stage and make their statement with the thoughtfulness of the design and materials used, and the play of scale and high-end textural finishes. "I often draw color inspiration from the surrounding landscape to blur the lines between indoors and outdoors and create a greater sense of connectivity with nature," says Robin. This was achieved with antique mirrored tiles that reflect the views. Architecture by Amy A. Alper, Architect

► **There's a trend of cabinetry getting lighter, including wood— more maple and light oak rather than very dark. What colors work well with that look?**

Colors that work well with lighter wood kitchens tend to be softer colors such as blue grays, softer sage greens, and neutrals like taupe and warm grays. This lighter design style is easier on the eyes and comes across as more casual. It eliminates high contrast, giving the room a friendlier atmosphere. This approach is not as trendy and bold. It's quite the opposite, creating a space in which you can relax at the beginning and end of every day.

► **How will natural versus artificial light from a certain direction affect the colors in a room?**

We spend a lot of time in the kitchen and the lighting in the room is extremely important for a few reasons. We want to have lighting that is easy on our eyes (not too harsh and bright), but a good balance so we can see clearly what we are doing. After all, it is a task-driven environment. We are working with sharp tools, so our work areas have to be well lit.

Kelvin is how we measure the brightness and color of our light bulbs. Most lighting ranges from 3000 to 5000 Kelvin. If you want a cozier illumination that feels like the traditional interior lighting in your other rooms, choose a bulb with 3000 Kelvin. If you want a brighter bulb, you can ratchet it up to 4000 or 4500. I would be less inclined to go higher than that. It might be a little too bright and tiring for your eyes.

What is the best light? Natural daylight is a win-win every time. It illuminates a room comfortably. Daylight in combination with illuminated work areas is ideal assuming the design of your rooms gives you that option.

Opposite In this
kitchen designed by
Susan Brunstrum, Studio
Brunstrum, light dove gray
perimeter cabinets contrast
handsomely with the blue
island, crisp white backsplash
tile, and white Forte Dei
Marmi quartz countertop slab.

▶ **What are your recommendations about floor colors?**

I generally like a floor that has some depth to it when it comes to color. Slate grays, warm wood tones, even darker tiles will add weight to the room. It also gives the cabinetry a chance to stand out and feel clean and bright against the contrasting floor. Lighter colors on the floor give the cabinetry a feeling like it's floating. The darker colors anchor the room and flow well visually from the other floors in adjacent rooms that lead into the kitchen.

▶ **How many different colors and materials are too many? Are there any rules on mixing colors when it comes to islands?**

The kitchen island is a distinctive opportunity to add color to your kitchen. Many designers generally steer away from color themes that are too heavy, bold, and overwhelming.

When it comes to choosing a color for the kitchen island, it's fair game. Popular colors of the island can be navy blue or rich charcoal, or even stained wood, adding warmth to the room.

A more dramatic approach would be to apply bolder colors to your island like a hunter green, teal blue, or even a striking black. It's important to keep in mind that the island needs to complement the cabinetry and not compete with it. I have talked about balance in designing a kitchen. This is where one element needs to take center stage with the other colors as a supporting cast. If the island is your statement piece in the kitchen, then your kitchen cabinets should not be as bold or colorful.

What I have always loved about adding color to the kitchen island is that if you change the color of the island, it's as if you have changed the personality of the whole room. In this context, choosing a color for your kitchen island is all about giving your kitchen a personal touch.

▶ **Does color need to be carried through from other rooms to the kitchen?**

The most successful way to design a new kitchen is to consider the flow of the space from the adjoining rooms to the brand-new kitchen. Not factoring the style of the home into the design of your kitchen will make it feel out of place and take away from the beauty of your new kitchen design.

If you want a design that takes advantage of updated features now available in kitchens that were not available when your home was built (and the list of updated features is endless), then use a similar color palette. It will bridge the gap between how your home is designed and when your new kitchen was designed and installed.

With an open floor plan, the design of the kitchen should visually flow from the surrounding rooms. It will be visible from many areas of your home. My suggestion would be to make less of a bold statement in the color palette you use in your new kitchen so it flows into the open space and complements the design of the surrounding areas in your home.

- **Does a home's style (e.g. midcentury modern, contemporary) factor into kitchen color choice(s)?**

  The most successful designs take the style of the home into consideration. You have the option of giving a nod to the original style of the home or going to great lengths to design a kitchen that feels like it was an original kitchen to the style and period of the home. Look at the period of your home, choose the colors you feel are like "home," and leave the other colors behind. If your home has craftsman features, you might want to include the terracottas and warm earth tones, but not include the heavy olives and dark browns typical of the period. Another suggestion is to look at the popular midcentury modern color palettes and choose the colors to which you are drawn. You might include in your design the teal–blues and slate–blue grays but leave behind the golds and olives, which can look very dated.

  If your home is contemporary, it would be appropriate to have the kitchen feel like (and look like) it was designed around the same time or to at least reflect the vibe of the original design. That does not mean it has to be an exact match, especially if your home is 20 or more years old. However, giving a nod to the original style with updated improvements will make the kitchen feel like it belongs there.

- **How do you keep a kitchen from looking dated if it's too expensive to remodel?**

  The easiest answer is to keep the colors classic and not trendy. Color trends come and go, and the best way to avoid falling into that ruse is to choose colors that you have loved for a very long time. For example, if you have always loved navy blue, then design your kitchen around a navy-blue palette.

This spread Natural sunlight in this loft enhances a blue wall divider made from reclaimed ash from Hudson Flooring with painted MDF panels. Designed by Andrew Franz, AIA, Andrew Franz Architect

Colors of hardware can update your kitchen if need be. Classic blue is a color that has been around for a long time and it's not going away soon. Another way to avoid problems with your kitchen going out of style is to look at your adjoining rooms. Do you have light wood and lots of white in the rooms surrounding your kitchen? If so, then a white kitchen would be appropriate—would not feel out of place and will stand the test of time.

Imagine yourself living with the colors you are considering for five, 10, or 15 years from now. Do you think you'll still love them just as much? That might influence your decision on how much or how little color to include in your design.

▶ **How can homeowners use color for a "cheap fix" to make cosmetic changes to their kitchen?**

I would suggest starting with painting the ceiling in your kitchen. If you have a white kitchen, imagine adding a light-blue ceiling, which will create an open and airy feeling to the room. Another approach is to paint the walls, adding a color that you truly love. Whether you have wood cabinets or white cabinets, imagine painting your walls a warm mocha or butterscotch color, adding warmth and personality to your space. It doesn't have to be a bold color. It can simply be a color to warm up the room to make a significant change.

Looking for something bolder to make a statement? Paint the walls an elegant and classic navy blue. It will add drama to your space. Also, it's a color that is practically neutral so it will complement any wood (or white) cabinetry. Paint colors are among the easiest and cheapest fixes if you tire of a hue.

TWO COOKS, ONE KITCHEN

In conversation with Studio Brunstrum

Chicago, Illinois-based interior design firm Studio Brunstrum transformed an outdated 20-year-old kitchen into a sophisticated, simple workspace that could accommodate more than one chef. The kitchen was 275 square feet—not overly large, as the home is in an urban condo. The rest of the home had been updated when the clients moved in six years earlier, so the designers created a kitchen that would feel cohesive within the home. They primarily worked within the existing footprint, moving only the south entry location to accommodate better traffic flow and enhance a view of Lake Michigan. They integrated the kitchen into the condo as a whole by complementing the color palettes of furniture, floors, rugs, wallpaper, and artwork.

To transform the space, Studio Brunstrum:

▸ added double ovens and a steam oven;

▸ created a coffee bar area;

▸ separated the upper and lower cabinets to maximize storage space;

▸ created closed storage to house the HVAC unit and revamp the pantry space;

▸ added USB ports underneath the seated side of the peninsula countertop to accommodate additional workspace when the clients' adult children visit;

▸ custom designed flexible drawer insets to organize an array of spices, oils, and utensils;

▸ selected three different cabinet finishes (a gray-blue lacquer on the fridge and dining room built-ins, a washed driftwood on the perimeter and seating peninsula, and a cream in the pantry) along with mixed metals throughout to add dimension;

▸ dropped a lighting soffit over the peninsula for three custom pendants to match the lacquer of the fridge and cladded the walls on the south side of the kitchen and into the pantry for continuity;

▸ added antique mirrors and antique glass above the sink and in the pantry for a touch of glamor;

▸ mirrored the simple routing on the cabinetry doors into metal detailing on the fridge; and

▸ opted for leather-wrapped hardware in the dining room inset cabinetry—the perfect finishing touch.

Cost: $405,000

Timeline: 15 months

Professionals involved: Studio Brunstrum spearheaded the project on behalf of the client, partnering closely with nuHaus cabinetry, an appliance retailer, and an independent contractor.

Best feature: The Calacatta Chiara (countertop, picture-framed backsplash, and base molding material) was the most problematic during installation but is easily the best feature in the kitchen; it took more than two weeks to diligently install, ensuring the veining in the quartzite was bookmatched and seamless throughout. The material was also used as a footer to balance out the narrow soffit and give the kitchen a crisp, clean look.

What sets it apart: The attention to detail in this project was astounding. The Studio Brunstrum team worked to make sure the kitchen was highly functional and efficient, while still maintaining quality design selections that fit with the rest of the home. The custom appliance garage at the north end was a must-have, allowing room for the nook above to house the clients' favorite sculpture. The use of antique mirror was a connecting element as well, so it was used for the backsplash of the great room bar.

Regrets: None

Lesson(s) learned: "Give yourself the time and budget to cover unexpected costs! Due to the new cabinetry layout in this project, the hardwood floor had to be filled in and living room, dining room, kitchen, and foyer floors had to be re-stained," says the design team.

CHAPTER 7

Lighting: Illuminating Your Kitchen, Indoors & Outdoors

Good lighting will add beauty, interest, function, and safety to your kitchen. It's a key ingredient that is much more important today because the room is used for all kinds of purposes and it functions as the center of the house—the workhorse and the hub. Additionally, technological advancements in lighting make it possible to achieve homeowners' desired effects.

More homeowners now realize its value for both function and aesthetics. They understand how lighting may help activate different moods and increase safety when they are wielding a knife, taking a hot pot off a range, or venturing into the room at night to grab a drink of water.

Lighting experts have been teaching the value of a lighting plan, in the same way that other professionals may develop a furnishings plan for each room and a garden plan for the outdoors even before they step into a store to buy merchandise of any kind. When lighting a kitchen, fixtures should be installed in multiple layers, all controlled from different switches for different amounts of lumens, the measure of the total amount of visible light from a light source.

THREE LAYERS OF LIGHT

Experts speak of three layers of light working together for best results:

▶ **Task:** Homeowners are smart to focus on the task lighting layer in a kitchen, which illuminates areas where work will be performed. It keeps hands safe and visible while slicing, measuring, simmering, and loading a dishwasher, among many other tasks.

▶ **Overall:** Then there's the need for overall or general lighting to showcase the entire room and make different zones come alive. It makes the kitchen pleasurable for lingering; otherwise, who would want to be there on a dreary winter day or after the sun has gone down? If the kitchen lacks good natural light from windows, skylights, and doors with glazing, artificial light from bulbs becomes the prime source.

▶ **Ambient:** The third layer creates the mood you want to achieve—bright and perky like a kitchen showroom, low-key and elegant like a classy restaurant with a hint of romance, or fun with different colors (known as "temperatures" in light lingo). The lights are not all white, and, as with paint, there are many variations.

Opposite In a traditional kitchen designed by Marina Case, The Red Shutters, old-style pendants and in-cabinet lighting show off a blue and white plate collection.

"When you walk into a room, rather than have one type [of light], you should have a variety of options, all individually controlled," says Joseph A. Rey-Barreau, AIA (the American Institute of Architects), IES (The Illuminating Engineering Society of North America), an architect, lighting designer, and associate professor. Larry Lauck of the American Lighting Association (ALA) adds, "Lighting can also be adjusted by time of day, so it goes from bright to a soft glow before bedtime when you may try to alter your circadian rhythms."

ADVANTAGES OF A LIGHT PLAN

Many designers are skilled at developing a lighting plan with solutions for different areas of the kitchen. Designer Marina Case includes lighting suggestions in her plans and elevations as part of her fee. Her contractor or electrician may fine-tune it based on fixtures and bulbs that will work best. They and other designers and architects know that different surfaces, materials, textures, and colors will reflect light differently, so the plan must take the variations into account. "A glossy white countertop might call for a fixture with one temperature while dark wood cabinets might dictate a different choice," Case says.

No matter how experienced designers (or architects) are in these choices, many will consult with an electrician or contractor who's knowledgeable about electricity. If the plan calls for more lighting, the electrician may recommend upgrading the electrical panel or wiring of the house.

Above William Ramsey, KTGY, and Kate Pourhassanian, Unscripted Interior Design, took special care to select materials and colors in this kitchen. Texture was paramount, blending smooth and rough, glossy and matte to blur the line between natural and artificial elements. Pendant lighting allows visual connections to the outdoors to remain unobstructed, respecting the home's connection to the surrounding environment.

Opposite In this kitchen designed by Fabrice Garson, Bilotta Kitchen & Home, good illumination comes from LED lighting inside glass-fronted wall cabinets, LED strips under the cabinets, LED pucks between sections of the coffered ceiling, simple yet elegant fixtures above the island, and a decorative fixture above the banquette.

In many cases, homeowners may also bring in a lighting consultant who knows the latest solutions. Some are certified and may be listed on the ALA's website (alalighting.com). The expert may work for a showroom, be affiliated with a college, or be an independent contractor. Most charge by project or hour. Some who work for a showroom may offer advice for free if a homeowner buys some merchandise.

Shawn Carstensen with Wolberg Lighting Design & Electrical Supply in Kingston, New York, likes potential clients to share how they want their kitchen to function and what light look they seek—perhaps a wide beam with soft glow, or a light effect that's crisp and focused.

Advice can also come from independent designers who are members of the International Association of Lighting Designers (IALD). "These professionals often charge by the hour but that may depend on the scope of the work they perform and where they work since different parts of the country have different rates," says Rey-Barreau. In hiring anyone, remember to inquire upfront about services and prices.

SEE POSSIBILITIES

Be on the lookout for showrooms that have what's called "a lighting lab" where different-looking rooms or a small furnished area demonstrate how different products and temperatures look and work in a real-life setting. Seeing such displays can help you make informed selections.

Opposite and above Floor-to-ceiling windows take advantage of natural light and sweeping views in the daytime and, at night, downlighting illuminates the kitchen to replicate daytime natural lighting. Designed by Christopher Grubb, Arch-Interiors Design Group

LEARN ABOUT LEDS

The good news in lighting kitchens and other rooms today is that all bulbs are apt to be much longer lasting and more energy-efficient light-emitting diodes (LEDs). These are small semiconductor devices that emit light when conducting an electrical current.

Initially very expensive, LED prices have come down dramatically. In fact, the United States Department of Energy says prices have fallen 90 percent since 2010. Nathan Kipnis, FAIA, LEED BD+C, sustainability expert, and owner of Kipnis Architecture + Planning (KAP), says the price of one bulb was $8 in 2008, but was $1.50 by 2022. At the same time, LEDs use up to 90 percent less energy and last up to 25 times longer than traditional incandescent bulbs.

That's not all. "Because of the small size of LEDs, it is now possible to insert them easily in specialized locations," says Rey-Barreau. They can go under cabinets in thin, linear, "rope" strips, above cabinets, inside cabinets, in toe kicks at the base of cabinets to help light a floor (a boon for older people and people with disabilities) and added in recessed cans in ceilings and walls and barely be visible. They help homeowners see light rather than the source. In the past, the ceiling style consisted of wide cans or apertures (the openings through which light moves) of six inches in diameter, which decreased over time and is now much smaller (three-, two-, or one-inch diameter options). "From those tiny holes, you can achieve a lot of light," says Rey-Barreau. One result of these smaller, more effective bulbs is a cleaner, less chopped-up looking ceiling.

Previous pages and this spread Feinmann, Inc. revitalized this kitchen by removing barriers to light and replacing them with full-height glass doors, transforming darkness into brilliance. The glass and metallic statement pendants above the island fuse classic form and cutting-edge technology into a dramatic focal point, commanding attention and admiration.

The lighting in the wine and coffee bar areas is carefully curated to evoke an ambiance of sophistication while illuminating the shelves; The walk-in pantry lighting ensures maximum visibility and accessibility, making it easy to locate ingredients and kitchen essentials; The desk area offers ambient down lighting, gently illuminating the workspace, ensuring that the desk remains a functional and welcoming space within the kitchen.

Besides the size of the bulb, a designer will suggest housings that might blend into the ceiling or stand out depending on the material and color chosen and the desired look. These can be fitted with baffles and lenses that block light to prevent glare or brightness.

"Color-producing LEDs are also available. Solutions may range from lower color temperatures measured in Kelvins (K), from 2700K in warmer oranges and yellows to 3000K, which is a purer white color temperature," Rey-Barreau says. "Temperatures go higher to 4000K and beyond, which have cooler blue tones of white light." Within the categories are many variations, including for whites. Color expert Amy Wax tries to stay under 4000K or 4500K for most rooms. "Otherwise, the light might be a little too bright and tiring on eyes," she says. "The best light solution also is a combination of any illuminated artificial light needed, plus daylight, assuming rooms offer that option."

Smart LED bulbs are all the rage. Change the color and intensity, incorporate speakers, or program them to turn on and off or go dim from a single switch, smartphone app, or remote control, or by voice. A homeowner can also have a light scene programmed to automatically turn on and off, even before they enter or leave a room of their house.

All LEDs may be dimmable but this requires the right technology to speak the same language as the bulb. "This [compatibility] is incredibly important, and many homeowners don't understand [the concept] since all incandescent lights were the same. Each LED is different," Rey-Barreau says. If the technology is incompatible and/or the wrong bulb is chosen, the dimmer may not work.

DECORATIVE DETAILS

Using the source of the light as a decorative focal point or accent has become more important to help personalize and style a kitchen. Solutions show up in a wide variety of sconces, chandeliers, pendants, ceiling-mounted designs, and ceiling fans with lights built into them. These choices help add punch to a kitchen through a mix of materials, colors, shapes, and sizes. And choices can be compatible with other design features from the style of cabinets to type of artwork on walls or furnishings.

Many design professionals and homeowners are using light choices in new fresh ways as a less rigid design environment gains traction. You don't have to keep to an all-traditional or modern look. It's become more commonplace to see fancy living- or dining-room style crystal chandeliers in a kitchen as Los Angeles, California, designer Christopher Grubb of Arch-Interiors Group has done.

Of late, fixtures have gotten larger, adding a dramatic focal point. The familiar style of three small lights above an island or table is being replaced by bolder choices or a single choice. Jodi Swartz of KitchenVisions likes to use some large lights over islands, including some linear designs. On the other hand, some effects can be more subtle, such as light aimed gently down a wall or up at a ceiling for a grazing effect, or several dimmed together for zone lighting.

You may wonder if there is such a thing as too much light. Yes, say some pundits, what's called "over-lamping." But one way to avoid that is with dimmers. For example, Rey-Barreau prefers to have the option of more lighting and not use everything all at once at all times but control how much.

Above Glass and polished nickel elements are a theme in the lighting and decorative shelving in this modern kitchen designed by Claire Staszak, Centered by Design, with stylist Jen DeCleene.

Opposite The addition of hammered brass petals on pendants is the perfect match to the brass range hood in this kitchen designed by Cheryl Kees Clendenon, In Detail Interiors.

Following pages William Caligari Interiors created both the kitchen and main light fixture, which has ceramic cowbell-shaped shades and metal parts sourced locally.

EXTERIOR LIGHTING

Outside, new lighting technology adds to enjoyment of an outdoor kitchen, dining area, and surrounding landscape. LED can be low or line voltage. The line voltage is the same 120 volts found inside but can be dangerous to work with outside and needs to be buried in the ground. "Low voltage is below thirty volts—often twelve to twenty-four—and much safer to work with and more flexible," says Rey-Barreau.

From a deck or terrace where you cook and eat, you can use lighting choices to landscape your surroundings, graze exterior surfaces, and bring out textures of the house material such as brick, the wood of a deck, or plant materials with rough or smooth surfaces by silhouetting trees and bushes, moonlighting plants, or a body of water, maybe with fish!

These lights, like those you use inside, can reflect the LED rainbow of hues. Your choices can also help make your property more secure and safe for night-time use, whether you cook, eat, stargaze, or make s'mores over a firepit. They also can help give you a feeling of safety if you program them to turn on and off if you're away from home for a night or longer period.

For any purposes, consult a lighting expert or a landscape designer or architect for where to place them and which to use. The extra expense will help you achieve the best results you can the first time and for the least cost. There won't be a need for do-overs.

ILLUMINATING DESIGN

In conversation with designer Annie Mandelkern and clients Janice & Jordan, Port Washington, New York

When a young couple, Janice and Jordan, bought a new builder home, the kitchen didn't reflect the same quality of space as the rest of the home. It also lacked natural and artificial light. The space needed a reset.

Interior designer Annie Mandelkern recalls Janice making an offhand comment to the design team: "If I knocked down a wall and put the range on the opposite wall and removed a maid's room, powder room, and mud room, I could gain a kitchen twice the size." The room would also be much lighter and brighter.

Architect Paul Russo, kitchen designer John Starck, and Mandelkern, the interior designer, all decided to do just that and then some. They installed windows on either side of the range, added a three-part window behind the sink with a transom above, and installed another window on the opposite side.

With those changes, the room didn't need a lot of artificial light—just some bulbs to illuminate areas for tasks and ambience after the sun goes down. Standard high hats with LEDs were added in the coffered ceiling and under many cabinets. To provide good lighting above the island and at the table, Mandelkern selected three oversized lanterns with a black trim, which added design consistency. "There are so many options today in decorative lighting, but my client felt overwhelmed and told me to pick. She was thrilled with the choice," Mandelkern says. All bulbs are on dimmers. The kitchen can now be bathed in natural and artificial light.

Other changes to the couple's space included:

▸ undergoing a complete gut renovation and relocation of spaces with high-end choices, including a 60-inch La Cornue range;

▸ adding two-inch-thick statuary marble on the island and 1¼-inch on countertops and behind the range;

▸ adding TuffSkin protection (which covers many cell phones) to the surfaces; and

▸ painting cabinets white in an inset style from Showcase Kitchens.

Budget: Over $100,000

Timeline: Approximately six months, and a race to get it finished before Janice and Jordan's baby was born.

Professionals involved: Annie Mandelkern, John Starck from Showcase Kitchens, and Paul Russo from Paul Russo Architect, PC.

Best feature: "A tie between the La Cornue range and the statuary marble countertops," Mandelkern says.

What sets it apart: "It's a large, open space with several designated areas: kitchen, breakfast room, side bar, and built-in bench/storage area," Mandelkern states.

Regrets: None

Lesson(s) learned: "Teamwork makes a kitchen vision work," Mandelkern says.

CHAPTER 8

The Kitchens of Tomorrow

No one yet can see the future, but technology and sustainability are two design tools already guiding kitchen design, and they will continue to do so.

TECHNOLOGY

Luddites, take note! Technology will be running our kitchens within the next three to five years. Features will be smart, efficient, hands off, sustainable, healthier, and safer. The high-tech trend will not preclude designing our kitchens to be beautiful, comfortable, and cozy, with nature-inspired themes and European trends, according to the *2023 Design Trends* report from the NKBA. There will be fewer tasks to do and more time to enjoy the people and world around us, as well as the food we or others prepare.

In fact, the kitchen of the future (KOF) might be right out of the Disney movie *Smart House* (1999), in which a computer-savvy child automates his home to make his family's life easier. But will our high-tech kitchens, outfitted with virtual projections and powered by artificial intelligence (AI) to learn our habits and behavior, develop minds of their own? If so, who knows where that might lead? Like it or not, use it or not, automation in the kitchen is here and ramping up. Once we master the technology, we'll simply press buttons, wave our hands, give voice commands or use facial recognition, show up, and eat. Eating, as far as we know, has not been automated … yet. Robots may be programmed to be a personal chef and serve, or even feed, us and then clean up. What a relief. If you think this sounds like science fiction, it is. What fun we'll have in the family's favorite hub as we head into a future where technology is a boon and lifesaver—with no negative side effects, we hope.

Michele Alfano, Michele Alfano Design, Montebello, New York wants to allay the fears you may have surrounding technology. She knows that technology scares some folks, especially the Boomer cohort, but touts its importance to serve our needs and solve problems. "Otherwise, it's just a nuisance and an expense," she says. "Once the consumer starts to learn that technology will impact lives with less waste, and less time in the kitchen, they'll embrace it. Good technology is sophisticated technology that just disappears in the background and allows you to feel like you have done something extraordinary. Let the technology work for you," Alfano advises. And it will.

Opposite This home designed by Morgante Wilson Architects is built to Passive House standards and includes a high level of insulation to minimize energy use. The kitchen is designed with energy-efficient appliances, such as an electric induction cooktop, that have the least impact on the home's interior temperature.

Glenn Rush, a design manager at Build with Ferguson, a website dedicated to home improvement fixtures, explains how technology works and fits together so the right hand, figuratively speaking, knows what the left hand is doing. This will be accomplished with an IoT (Internet of Things), which creates a large network of connected items through your Wi-Fi—a hub, if you will—such as the oven, fridge, dishwasher, and faucet. All of these collect and share data about how you use the devices, and then they communicate with each other.

Setting up the IoT network might not be in everyone's wheelhouse. Always read the instructions that come with each device. If you need more help, try Google or YouTube, or ask your contractor or design team, a computer guru or—when all else fails—a teenager!

Automation is good for safety's sake. It will have the capability to stop a problem in its tracks. For example, if someone forgets to turn off a faucet at the sink, the faucet will automatically shut off at a certain point to avoid flooding the room and wasting water. This is useful for the older community who may be forgetful, or for people with disabilities who may greatly benefit from voice commands.

The NKBA *2023 Design Trends* report cites upcoming smart trends:

▶ **Exciting kitchen technology**
- Faucet controls (touchless, motion sensor, voice-activated, and/or touch-free operation pre-filling amounts)
- App/mobile/voice controls (app/smartphone/tablet/mobile device, voice control)
- Cooking appliances (steam oven, air fryer, induction cooktop)
- Lighting/LEDs (voice activated controls, under cabinet)
- Charging/power (charging stations/drawers, hidden outlets)
- Smart/high-tech appliances (integrated, voice activated)
- Smart refrigerator (inventory control, meal ideas, touch screen)
- Water filtration
- Coffee/wine dispenser

Above (left to right)
MasterBrand Cabinets will ensure the future is simple and free of clutter with these three innovative ideas. Cleanup will be a breeze with the Toekick vacuum cabinet by Diamond® Cabinets; Toekick drawers from Omega Cabinetry add an unexpected new storage area; No searching for nearby outlets needed with the Power Pod by Decorá.

Following pages Flat panel white gloss cabinets, Miele's Brilliant White appliances, white Corian® countertops, and an integrated Corian® sink with a mirrored backsplash that doubles the light to increase the impression of spaciousness gives a contemporary kitchen futuristic flair in this urban penthouse. Designed by Regina Bilotta, Bilotta Kitchen & Home, with Jennifer Post, Jennifer Post Design

- ▶ **Prominent kitchen technology**
  - Steam-cooking/air-frying tech integrated into ovens
  - Dedicated areas for device charging and viewing
  - Mobile app to control appliances, and voice-activated appliances
  - Open refrigerator door detector/mobile alert
  - Technology that supports precision cooking
  - Taps that elevate water purity and convenience
  - Integrated speakers/audio system
  - Smudge-proof internet touch screens/tablets for meal ideas and recipes
  - Wall-mounted screens/monitors and/or touch panel interfaces
  - Technology that facilitates seamless video communication with friends/family/work
  - Wine dispensers

- ▶ **Kitchen safety & emerging technology**
  - Automatic leak/flood detector/mobile alert
  - Electric power failure or gas leak detector/mobile alert
  - Refrigerator emergency power source
  - Alarm safety

Before considering any of these, Rush advises checking with your architect, kitchen designer, contractor, plumber, or electrician to make sure your house can handle the technology load. If not, you may first need to update your wiring and electric panel.

Technology is only one part of the kitchen of the future snapshot, however. Contrary to what you may think, it is not imperative to embrace an ultra-modern décor and let technology upstage your personal taste. Capitalize on the fact that you can choose colors, finishes, and materials that can give smart appliances a personalized look, notes Sara Malek Barney, ASID, founder and principal designer of Bandd/Design in Austin, Texas. "Our future kitchens will be a space that performs to its highest potential to have everything to get the job done but will contain enough elements of comfort and coziness for it to remain the heart of the home," Barney says. When Barney pictures a high-performance kitchen years from now, she says, "I immediately envision technologically advanced appliances and features, an abundance of storage, new hygienic solutions, and the perfect balance of safety, function, and overall aesthetic." What could be a better mix?

Why, when kitchens have been pretty similar for years, with variations in color of cabinets, backsplash tiles, and countertops, are these big changes coming now? Barney believes some of the new and future elements in our kitchen can be attributed to the Covid pandemic when home cooking became more essential, and people became more cognizant of keeping away germs. There's now greater interest in materials that are easy to clean and use. "Antimicrobial surfaces reduce offensive odors and stain-causing bacteria. Hands-off technology will be the norm," Barney says, adding, "At the same time, homeowners around the world are upgrading their kitchen layouts and appliances to create the most functional spaces."

This spread This kitchen, in a house with architecture and interiors designed by The Turett Collaborative: Architects and Interior Designers, follows Passive House standards with such elements as an induction cooktop and wood and metal cabinets.

But for those who want to put technology front and center in their kitchens, a sleek, contemporary design might one day resemble a spaceship, with angles and curves of cabinets and islands not unlike the exterior of Walt Disney Concert Hall in Los Angeles, designed by Canadian American architect Frank Gehry. Futuristic ideas in kitchen design abound. Rush saw many when he closely followed the building of the House of the Retro Future at the Howard Johnson Anaheim Hotel and Water Playground, designed in 2022 in Anaheim, California. It was heavily influenced by the Monsanto House of the Future, featured in Tomorrowland at Disneyland Park that closed in 1967. Rush says there are round islands with suspended hoods so someone could cook and see from any angle in the home. There is lighting that turns on automatically on the breakfast side of the kitchen and, in the evening, on the dinner side. "It is like harnessing the environment in a thoughtful way to bring it fully into your home," Rush says.

Other futuristic features might include integrated cabinets, those in unstandardized sizes, and ones that might stretch from ceiling to floor. Islands could be serpentine in shape and range hoods may look like lighting fixtures, integrated architectural elements, or a submarine periscope to create a nautical aesthetic. When it comes to melding automation with sustainability and other homeowner design choices, the possibilities are limitless.

SUSTAINABILITY

As the demand for technology heats up—much like the planet—we have entered an age of sustainability. Likely options in future kitchen design are all-electric kitchens and appliances (some smart) that use less energy, lower our carbon footprint, and may even include solar- and wind-powered technologies that are likely to steamroll fossil-fuel equivalents at some point.

The concept of sustainability might not roll off the tongue yet for everyone, but its time has come, with so many choices percolating now. Architect Nathan Kipnis, based in Evanston, Illinois, and Boulder, Colorado, is a proponent of sustainable and high-performance homes and kitchens. Kipnis says, "We want not only our designs to be extremely high performance, healthier, more efficient both in their operational carbon (HVAC system, lighting, refrigeration, and so on) as well as their 'embodied carbon,' which is the carbon needed to extract, transport, process, and install the actual materials, but to be beautiful as well."

This cultural shift is happening for a reason. In part, the increased interest in sustainability is an aftermath of the pandemic. It made us hyper-focused on our environment, health, and cleanliness with our gallons of hand sanitizer, incessant hand washing, and scrubbing everything down, including our groceries and mail. Special air purifiers and ventilation systems gained popularity in a slow transformation to cleanse the air of germs and toxic fumes in our homes and especially our kitchens, where we gather the most.

Dr Gernot Wagner, a climate economist at Columbia Business School, wrote in a *New York Times* article "Greening Your Home Will Be Cheaper, but Expect Growing Pains" on August 12, 2022, that the Inflation Reduction Act (2022) should be credited for bringing the need to be sustainable to the fore. And that's not surprising. If you are about to design your kitchen, you may be starting to consider sustainability a priority—but there's still work to be done.

Will sustainability become the norm in the near future? Kipnis says we are moving in that direction. In the past, he notes, about 50 percent of his clients specifically asked for sustainable design, probably in part because he's gained a reputation for being an advocate and knowing how to incorporate it. Now, as the threat of climate change looms bigger and has become clearer, that percentage has significantly increased, to around 80 percent, he says. "I think people understand that they are making the large investment in their lives ..."

Betsy Littrell, eco-architect, REALTOR® (RA, GREEN), and founder of Maypop Building Workshop, concedes that sustainable design is an evolving marketplace and still more fringe than focus. So, who's on board? Kipnis believes that millennials are more educated about sustainability and climate change than boomers. "They are also much more invested as they are the ones that have to deal with this over their entire life. Having said that, there are plenty of boomers that completely understand what is at stake and want to make the correct choices." They also have more capital to spend as costs rise. Littrell agrees that many millennials passionately support solutions that can reduce (and/or reverse) climate change and are willing to modify their behaviors. "Outside of millennial support, many Gen X and boomers are also very interested in sustainable projects because of how climate change is threatening the long-term livelihood for their children and grandchildren," she says.

Architects, designers, real estate practitioners, and brokers are starting to jump on the sustainable bandwagon to raise their clients' awareness about the importance of going green. Some real estate agents are signing up for the GREEN Designation program, run by the NAR, to become certified in energy efficiency and all that entails. This course also covers related costs and how to calculate the cash value of certain sustainable systems (factoring in tax credits and rebates), such as solar and geothermal systems. "Low carbon, high performance projects are design solutions that solve the most problems at once," says Littrell. "They use modern, plant-based materials to store *embodied carbon* in the building's materials while achieving low *operating carbon* through the building's resource efficiency. And as a bonus, these healthy materials translate to premium indoor air quality and are job-site friendly for the crew."

Kipnis is spreading the green gospel in Boulder, where he has opened an office. "It's an area where it's required by code to design to net-zero standards (achieving a balance between the carbon emitted into the atmosphere and the carbon removed from it) along with many other requirements for sustainable, resilient, and healthy homes. Homeowners also really value good design there, so it fits perfectly with our 'High Design/Low Carbon™' approach."

But how do you find a sustainable expert for your kitchen? Is there an organization? What credentials should that expert have? There are a number of places to look. Check references from previous projects. Look for awards relative to sustainable design from reputable institutions like the American Institute of Architects (AIA). Look for certifications from the U.S. Green Building Council's (USGBC) LEED certification, Passive House Institute/US (PHIUS), WELL, National Association of REALTORS® (NAR), and NKBA certification at the very least.

Littrell says the biggest hurdle to sustainable design is to find a project team that "gets it and works together to find sustainable solutions that work within real-world parameters of project budgets, vendor procurement, and local subcontractor skill sets and availability." Without this, she says, trying to pull off a sustainable project will be more costly, chaotic, and emotionally consumptive. "It's not easy, but sustainability-focused REALTORS®, architects/designers, and builders can help navigate these hurdles and streamline the process."

BETSY LITTRELL'S TOP SUSTAINABLE FEATURES IN A NEW OR REMODELED KITCHEN

- ▶ Eco-friendly and VOC-free cleaning products for healthy indoor air quality
- ▶ High-quality water filter (ideal for the whole house, and especially for drinking water at the sink)
- ▶ Infrastructure for composting and recycling
- ▶ Indoor and/or outdoor kitchen gardens to provide fresh, nutritious produce and reduce your carbon footprint
- ▶ Energy-efficient appliances (Energy Star® certified); dishwashers save both electricity and water
- ▶ Energy-efficient light fixtures; LED fixtures with coordinating color temperatures on dimmer switches offer dynamic task and mood lighting solutions
- ▶ Low-flow kitchen sink faucet
- ▶ Formaldehyde-free cabinets (hardwood or MDF)
- ▶ Eco-friendly countertop materials, such as:
  - Recycled glass, recycled paper, and quartz slabs using waste quartz materials, which are great options that marry performance, function, and sustainability
  - Recycled and FSC-certified wood countertops, which are sustainable and beautiful but require more maintenance and care.
- ▶ Proper ventilation—direct vent range hoods can exhaust pollutants to the exterior and should ventilate at a rate that matches the stove/range venting requirements. Dedicated makeup (additional) air may be required pending the volume and rate of air exhausted by the hood and should work in concert with a holistic HVAC system design for the home.
- ▶ Sustainable flooring that can be FSC-certified hardwoods, plant-based resilient flooring (such as Marmoleum), and floor tiles sourced from sustainable manufacturers, which are durable and offer design-flexible options.
- ▶ An induction cooktop over a gas range for enhanced cooking control, energy efficiency, and to eliminate harmful pollutants that are the byproduct of open flames. More important are the larger environmental concerns associated with natural gas (fracking, groundwater pollution, and failing infrastructure).

To learn about state-by-state incentives for renewables and energy efficiency, check out www.Dsireusa.org. It lists organizations to contact and ways to go solar. The Federal site is www.energy.gov/eere/solar/homeowners-guide-federal-tax-credit-solar-photovoltaics. Local power providers often have efficiency-related programs that may help finance efficient HVAC, electrical, and plumbing equipment, appliances, and lighting.

Littrell cautions that some professionals with the trade associations who have certification may not necessarily be versed on sustainable options.

Kipnis recommends doing your research. Be vigilant and wary. "One of the worst things out there are firms claiming to be providing sustainable work and/or products. This is known as 'greenwashing' and there is a lot of it out there. It usually carries a tinge of truth in the description, but the marketing department goes out of their way to exaggerate how good a product or service is. To be fair, it may take quite a while to transition a product or a service over to being fully sustainable," he says.

Real estate practitioner Christopher Matos-Rogers is certified in sustainable design by EarthCraft, a residential regional green building program in Atlanta that serves the Southeast. Matos-Rogers is a former marine biologist who saw firsthand how carbon impacts our oceans. When he and his husband, Heroildo, a database architect, moved to Atlanta, they bought a midcentury house that they converted into an all-electric home, with EarthCraft's guidance. This included an electric pump water heater that uses one-fifth the energy of a conventional natural gas or liquid propane design and saves on water usage. The couple made other sustainable tweaks in their lower-level kitchen, such as installing an induction oven and LED lighting with smart controls.

As his interest in sustainability grew, Matos-Rogers formed a team at his realty office to increase awareness of the advantages. Being green is always on his mind when he shows properties. "As a rule, my clientele does have the ability and willingness to pay for quality, long-lasting materials that might cost more upfront but are less expensive to operate. I help them create a roadmap of ways to improve their sustainability in a new kitchen, for example. They are excited at the prospect of lower bills, better performance of the equipment, and better air quality," he says, and adds the fact that sustainable options tend to extend the longevity of building parts and systems too. Another bonus.

The NKBA in its *2023 Design Trends* report thinks there's more awareness about sustainability and cites the most likely trends over the next three years.

▶ **Exclusively LED lighting:** Move over halogen bulbs because LEDs (light-emitting diodes) are illuminating more kitchens. They are more energy efficient with an expected lifespan 10,000 hours over conventional incandescent bulbs. The lightbulbs can be controlled by either a sensor, switch, app, voice activation, or remote-control device. To add glamor and drama to the kitchen, there are smart bulbs that change color and intensity and are high tech, programmed to turn on and off. Be sure the dimmer control and bulb are in sync to work properly.

▶ **Storage:** Dedicated recycling and composting areas are becoming the norm. A pull-out cabinet houses the trash can as well as containers for recyclable cans and compost.

▶ **Energy-efficient appliances:** United States Environmental Protection Agency (EPA) Energy Star®-certified appliances—refrigerators, freezers, ovens, and dishwashers—use significantly less energy than older appliances thanks to modern technology. Energy-efficient appliances are purposely designed to use as little energy as possible, while still functioning well.

Above Synergy Design & Construction balances the four elements in this unique kitchen remodel by using a water-esque backsplash, fireplace in the island, metal in the furnishings, and earth tones throughout.

If your current appliances are in good shape, it's sustainable to keep them. It keeps them out of landfill and will keep your costs down. If you don't want them, give them to a homeowner in need. Induction cooktops are more efficient than traditional stovetops, offer significant health and environmental benefits, and are easy to clean. Cast iron and other pots and pans that contain magnetic metals can be used for this type of cooking but aluminum, anodized aluminum, copper (Revere Ware, for example), glass, ceramic, silicone, and stainless steel are not recommended. For homeowners concerned about indoor air quality, burning fossil fuels such as gas in your kitchen isn't a great idea.

▶ **Power sources/systems:** Geothermal and solar systems are two sustainable engineering examples being used already by homeowners.

▶ **VOCs:** These volatile organic compounds should be eliminated and replaced with sustainable VOC-free coatings, VOC-free or low-VOC paints and stains, lacquers, paint strippers, building materials, and other furnishings used for countertops, cabinets, and flooring.

▶ **Recycled (reclaimed) materials:** Items made from reclaimed wood and other natural materials convey the impression of being at one with nature. They make better use of what's old and reuse it rather than dump it in landfill.

- ▶ **Windows:** High-performance low-E (low-intensity) triple-glazed glass windows and doors minimize infrared and ultraviolet light coming through the glass and don't pare natural light. They offer better insulation, block exterior heat, cold and humidity and, on this basis, cut energy use.
- ▶ **US EPA WaterSense faucets and fixtures:** These use 20 percent less water than Federal water-efficiency requirements, which saves money and wastes less water. There are rebates available if you use these fixtures.
- ▶ **VOC-free flooring:** These are made from recycled materials such as cork, linoleum, vinyl, bamboo, glass, and concrete.
- ▶ **HVAC:** Mechanical ventilation with a heat recovery system and alternative, energy-efficient water heaters are both sustainable. Tankless water heaters are known as "demand heaters" because you turn them on and there is instantaneous hot or cold water. Heat pump water heaters use heat from the ambient air to heat your water. They are perhaps the most efficient ones on the market, utilizing up to 60 percent less energy compared to a conventional water heater. Solar water heaters are heated by the sun. Condensing water heaters get their heat from the hot exhaust gases that would otherwise escape your household through flues.
- ▶ **Countertops:** Sustainable choices include quartz rather than engineered choices, unless they're made from recycled materials like aluminum scrap, post-industrial plastics, colored glass, quartzite, and even recycled paper composites.

For smart waste disposal ideas, go to: www.bigrentz.com/blog/smart-waste-management

CHRISTOPHER MATOS-ROGERS' FUTURE KITCHEN PLAN

At some point in the near future, EarthCraft-certified sustainable designer Christopher Matos-Rogers and his husband Heroildo will build a full-blown sustainable kitchen on the terrace level of their home in Atlanta, Georgia. The couple already has an electric pump water heater that uses one-fifth the energy of a conventional natural gas or liquid propane design and saves on water usage.

Matos-Rogers' future vision incorporates these changes:

- ▶ Opening up the space and taking everything in the kitchen back to the studs
- ▶ Making electrical changes so they can use additional automation in that part of their house
- ▶ Installing quartz countertops
- ▶ Minimizing resources by installing open shelves, which is more cost effective
- ▶ Installing solid wood cabinets with low VOCs that will last 50 to 100 years—far beyond their ownership
- ▶ Incorporating local red oak hardwood floors with low VOCs
- ▶ Adding filtered ventilation that does not recirculate air but instead sends it outside and brings in fresh air continuously
- ▶ Switching out windows to long-lasting Energy Star® fiberglass, which does not need to be painted and doesn't conduct heat or attract cold

MICHELE ALFANO'S KITCHEN OF THE FUTURE—MIND, HEART, BODY, & EARTH

Interior designer Michele Alfano, of Michele Alfano Design LLC, Montebello, New York, predicts that the components of a dream kitchen of the future can be organized into four categories. The combination of technology and nature creates a self-sustainable, healthy living space.

MIND: The design includes smart technology to make our lives easier and promote healthy living. Smart technology choices include the following:

- **Smart surfaces:** The smart counter is designed to respond to our needs in real time. The smart induction surface will have sensor technology that can learn our likes and our routines and assist us with everything.

- **Smart glass wall (projected mountain landscape):** The smart glass wall is either connected by voice recognition or connected back to our counters and information will be projected onto the glass. The wall recognizes who you are and has the ability to show video chats, recipes, your schedule for the day, emails, the weather, the time, and different landscapes.

- **Circadian:** A large expanse of glass immerses the kitchen space in natural light. Circadian lighting increases productivity and promotes better sleep.

- **Smart appliances:** Appliances through gestures or voice recognition will learn about you, your habits, and your behaviors to help you to cook more efficiently. Smart tech will control appliances to your liking, which will ultimately improve your cooking experience. A filtered kitchen faucet is essential to every health-conscious home. One company's faucet is engineered to provide easy access to safe, clean drinking water at the push of a button. The faucet delivers fresh, filtered water and regular tap water from a single, easy-to-install faucet. This environmentally friendly solution eliminates reliance on plastic water bottles. It has a sleek design that serves as a work of art in the space.

HEART: The design of the cabinetry, dual island, and see-through fireplace allows family and friends to come together to experiment, build, play, and be creative.

BODY: The development of ecosystems in the home brings people closer to nature and good nutrition. The design integrates home harvesting with a hydroponic system in the island to grow herbs year-round.

EARTH: The use of sustainable materials allows homeowners to give back to the planet. The design incorporates a sustainable countertop and ash timber materials with the least negative impact on the environment, as well as a compost area on the island to store waste that can be reused for the indoor farm.

- **Cabinets:** Keep your existing kitchen cabinets if they are in good shape by sanding, repainting, resurfacing, resealing, and refacing them, rather than tossing them away and starting over. This keeps them out of landfill—unless you choose to sell or donate them. Doing so will lower your kitchen design costs greatly since many cabinets represent 40 to 60 percent of the cost of redoing a kitchen. For new cabinets, consider formaldehyde-free MDF cabinets, cabinets that are certified by the FSC (Forest Stewardship Council), or those made from salvaged or local wood. Bamboo is considered a rapidly renewable resource, and, in kitchen cabinetry, its veneers are cut using ultra-thin slices of wood, so you get more bang for your buck.
- **Waste disposal:** A biodigester is a container made from various materials that acts as an electric stomach. It ferments organic waste from humans and animals to produce fertilizer.

HOW MUCH DOES IT ALL COST?

Do you need to be rich to be sustainable, which many fear? Not necessarily. "If you're doing one element of a kitchen, the 'sustainable' option may cost more, but if you're doing a whole-kitchen remodel and/or new home, spending more money on formaldehyde-free cabinets can be offset by saving money on a budget-friendly tile, and so on," Littrell says.

Kipnis says the price isn't as significant as people sometimes think. Many of the specialty sustainable items are now standard or mandated, he says. And it's just common sense to go green. "If you design a tight home with a sustainable kitchen, you aren't going to want to have a gas cooktop that spews out CO_2 and particulates into your home." He adds that savings are in energy efficiency, and it's important not to ignore the benefits of tax credits and rebates for sustainable items such as solar panels and Energy Star® appliances.

RESALE VALUE—DOES IT EXIST?

What about the resale value of a home with a sustainable kitchen as well as these features throughout the home? Real estate expert and green guru Matos-Rogers points out that the most sustainable kitchens will be the best kitchens you will see. "They use high-quality products that are designed to last. It takes only one person to love your home—or kitchen—and that is why it's important to have a (real estate) practitioner who is savvy about sustainability," he says. With such incentives, what's to stop you from going green? It can be the gift that keeps on giving—on many levels.

FORECAST FOR THE KITCHENS OF THE FUTURE

Kitchen pros Michele Alfano, Sara Malek Barney, and Glenn Rush—all prognosticators on the cutting edge of design—discuss what's here now and on the horizon for the future. They make it clear that high tech and personal design preferences will work in sync, save time, and permit us to enjoy other pursuits through the greater use of technology.

► **Colors**

Alfano: Warm tones, like camels, combined with hues of olive green, will infuse our spaces. The best source of inspiration is a palette from nature.

Barney: All-white kitchens are passé, but people aren't trying to go too bold with their color palettes, either. We will see a lot of natural, relaxing colors, such as tan, gray, and beige, as well as soft colors like light blues and greens on walls and cabinets.

► **Cupboards & shelving**

Alfano: Storage is becoming more important than open shelving. Coffee bars, breakfast pantry, and a separate butler's pantry would be ideal. On materials for cupboards, I predict natural woods combined with textured vinyl on the face of cabinetry, since vinyl is easy to wipe down and clean.

Barney: I think we will still see a combination of storage and a mix of design elements. However, they may be sleeker and more eco-friendly. On materials for cupboards, I see natural materials and more smooth fronts with no knobs for a streamlined look.

Rush: More pull-down cabinets. Each cupboard will serve a specific use, which will help with accessibility for anyone living with disabilities or aging in place. Technology might inventory items in cabinets. There will be lighting inside cabinets (in thin LED linear strips) when they're open and automatic closing systems. I envision a lot of synthetic surfaces that look good and are sustainable. Plant-based plastics and wood will be used. Craftmanship will resurface in wood cabinet designs.

► **Backsplashes**

Alfano: I predict backsplashes will turn into glass with differential textures to allow more natural lighting into spaces. Further into the future, glass backsplashes will become more interactive and act as screens to display emails, chats, zooms, family pictures, and recipes.

Barney: Backsplashes will always be part of the design but [will be] more elegant and streamlined.

Rush: Thinly cut, translucent stone or glass over an LED grid will be used as an additional source of light.

► **Islands**

Alfano: Dual-zoned islands. One island will be a workstation and a separate station will be dedicated to cooking, cleaning, and prepping. This is already happening in larger kitchens.

Opposite Jennifer Robin, Jennifer Robin Interiors, uses a marble island to provide an elegant entertaining space and a walnut center island perfect for cooking prep. "The surrounding countertops are honed black granite, chosen for its stain resistance and durability," says Robin. Architecture by Wade Design Architects

Barney: With their additional storage opportunities, islands will continue to be a staple in kitchen design. I think the designs will become more artful, such as using bright colors, tiles, and upscale details.

Rush: Islands are here to stay as the center of the kitchen. They offer flexibility. The possibilities of what they can hold are endless. Some will have straight storage, food attached to it with refrigeration, different shapes and sizes—maybe two islands if there's room in the space.

► **Countertops**

Alfano: Antibacterial counters will be more prevalent.

Barney: Nonporous surfaces like glass and metal.

Rush: Sustainable materials will be the focus. Reclaimed materials will be recycled in a beautiful way—like terrazzo, which can be a composite of ground-up plastics, glass, concrete, marble, and colored stone.

▶ **Hardware**

Alfano: Less hardware, more touch-to-open integral pulls.
Barney: While designs may be using less front hardware, there will still be room for specialty hardware and highlighted details.
Rush: Seeing two trends: statement hardware and disappearing hardware. Easy-to-grab hardware for accessibility, easy to clean, and nothing that will catch on[to] your clothes that can cause an accident.

▶ **Ovens, microwaves, stoves, & cooktops**

Alfano: Ovens will become more versatile and will do more than just convection by including sous vide, steam, and microwave options.
Barney: Easy-to-clean appliances will be a big selling point. Say goodbye to gas stovetops, and hello to induction stovetops that you can easily wipe clean. The trend has already started.
Rush: There will be options for accessibility, such as French-door ovens versus pull-down drawers. Also, combination ovens that are microwaves, convection, air fryers; in other words, which do it all. Single microwaves might be outdated. As for cooktops, induction again. It's easier to clean and as soon as you turn it off, it's cool to the touch, making it safer. And it's sustainable; it uses less energy because it cooks faster.

This spread Cabinet fronts, backsplash, and countertops are all crafted from dark sustainable ceramic and are complemented by the warm wood tones, creating a timeless kitchen space designed by 210 Design House.

Following pages Even in a very modern futuristic kitchen designed by Jean Liu Design, comfortable seating is critical; here, an upholstered banquette and chairs with a big table to gather.

- **Dishwashers**

  Alfano: From the pandemic, there was a rise in demand for dishwashers as people started to cook more at home. Companies are looking to enhance their functionality and dishwasher organization. Reconfigurable racks that tilt or collapse for small and oversized trays are a helpful way to tailor the dishwasher to what you need to load and clean.

  Rush: They are becoming more efficient. Instead of running long cycles, there will be sensors on dirty water lines to stop the cycle when the dishes are clean. This will save water and energy.

- **Sinks, faucets, & drains**

  Alfano: In sinks, seamless drains address unsightly germ rings around drains. In faucets, hands-free automation helps prevent the spread of germs. Voice activation will become more popular.

  Barney: We'll most likely see more large, open sinks to accommodate larger pans. Also, the addition of prep sinks to multitask.

  Rush: More workstation sinks.

- **Refrigerators**

  Alfano: I love that our refrigerators can talk to us through our phones. Smartphone apps have saved the day by alerting users remotely that they have left the door open or need to control the temperature. I think due to AI learning, the next refrigerator generation will offer recipes based on the contents of their fridge.

  Barney: They will continue to be efficient; we'll see more interior organization and, of course, technology.

  Rush: More column refrigerators or single-purpose refrigerators. Same with freezers. Putting fridges and freezers in separate locations can make sense. Maybe, freezers will go into the growing number of walk-in pantries.

- **Outlets & wiring**

  Alfano: We will see more concealed outlets integrated into our counters and backsplashes to meet ground-fault circuit interrupter codes, a fast-acting circuit breaker that shuts off electricity.

  Rush: A lot of companies that make outlets are aware their products are used to retrofit. It's recommended if you have old wiring, to upgrade and ground it. It uses less energy. Some appliances will use less energy because they'll have automatic controls that will shut them off when the right amount of energy has been used for the task at hand.

- **Docking stations & workstations**

  Alfano: Clutter be gone. Kitchens will be designed around a central workstation where one can prep, cook, serve, entertain, and clean. Operating as a hub instead of getting your bowls and boards from multiple shelves. So much more efficient.

  Rush: Customized landing spots for keys and phones are becoming more common. We'll see more specific stations such as a beverage station with hot-water dispenser and more niche areas, like a tea or coffee station. Lighting and fixture controls you will wave your hand at or tell it what to do if your hands are wet. It's a safety feature, too, especially for young kids and the elderly.

- **Offices**

  Alfano: More idea-sharing and creativity will overlap into our kitchens, especially thoughtfully designed butler's pantries with office nooks.

  Rush: Yes, but that's dependent on the size and flexibility of the space. We'll see more flexible spaces and more focus on soft architecture, flexing the space to whatever need you have that day. This can be walls and tables that move.

- **Seating**

  Alfano: Islands are becoming more curvilinear as more people embrace the organic trend. Expect to see more curved island benches.

  Barney: More natural materials and different blends of those materials will continue.

  Rush: Modular seating.

Above (left) A hidden storage feature with a sliding wall of Snow White and Afyon White Baby Picket Marble tile allows the homeowner to neatly conceal pantry items and small appliances in this kitchen designed by Feinmann, Inc. **(right)** Designer Susan Brunstrum from Studio Brunstrum knows that, in a condo kitchen, it is important to use all available space for storage, including a cabinet that lifts up, hiding what's inside.

▶ **Storage optimization**

Alfano: The thickness of porcelain slab has allowed for new storage solutions integrated into backsplashes … perhaps a new way to hide outlets and paper towel rolls.

Barney: Kitchen storage is, and will continue to be, of the utmost importance to every homeowner. Getting rid of upper kitchen cabinetry altogether has been a growing trend, however. An alternative to this is hidden (or disappearing) upper cabinet systems that benefit the aesthetic of the kitchen, while maintaining adequate storage space.

Rush: Hidden storage might be a door that you put in the back of the pantry attached to the garage so when you unload the car you can put groceries right into the pantry.

▶ **Ventilation & filtration systems**

Alfano: Clean air and ventilation will become increasingly important in our kitchens. Hood companies will start to produce futuristic designs to make a statement in our kitchens.

Barney: We're seeing a lot of filtration systems these days and I believe they will continue to evolve.

Rush: Especially after Covid, we started to see UV cleaning and reverse osmosis systems. Your home is the most polluted place, so it's important to have proper air filtration to eliminate pet dander, dust, and more. This will contribute to better health.

Above This kitchen designed by Nicole Ellis Semple, AIA, and Scott Rappe, AIA, Semple + Rappe Architects, makes sure that everything is easily accessible at the square island that includes seating for six, hidden storage, and multiple appliances.

► **Lighting**

Alfano: Interior lighting affects our body's internal clock and therefore how we sleep. Lighting companies are now focusing more on lighting systems based on our circadian rhythms.

Barney: I think pendant lighting will never go out of style. Metallic lighting designs have become a new style favorite, and I believe will carry on into the future.

Rush: Programmed lighting will be more of an item; some have it now. Lighting design systems consider sunlight and output from fixtures to give you the perfect mood throughout the day.

► **Window coverings**

Alfano: Predict seeing more window coverings hidden in ceilings and activated on an app to come down, and then go up.

Rush: Any room the sun touches makes it a good place to use solar energy. Coverings can be programmed with the lighting to work together.

- **Sound systems**

  Alfano: Music that seemingly comes from nowhere is the next best thing. Companies are developing speakers that are hidden behind the sheet rock, and your spaces can be filled with music without any visible signs of a speaker. 'Yes!' to less Swiss cheese in our ceilings.

  Barney: Sound systems [in the kitchen] are definitely becoming more popular. It's up to a designer to bring out that added feature or character into a design.

  Rush: Integrated stereo. It's one of the great joys in life.

- **Demographics**

  Alfano: Since the 1940s we have been using the work triangle as a design principle to design kitchens. The refrigerator–sink–stove triangle where three functions in a kitchen (food storage, cooking/prep, and cleanup) had to be within four feet and nine feet of each other to result in the most efficient completion of cooking tasks. Guess what? I think that work triangle is going away. The modern kitchen needs more touch points like a homework/work zone, and a breakfast or snack zone besides prepping/cooking, gathering, and eating. My thought is that the 'work triangle' is going to start to look more like a 'work pentagon.' Taking on more functions in the kitchen will require the modern kitchen to rely on a new design principle.

  Barney: I think families will embrace different aspects of technology along with thinking of kitchens as more of the hub rather than just for cooking and eating. The trend already started during the pandemic as more gathered there to socialize, do work, and pay bills.

  Rush: Not limited to any age group but depends on what works for each family.

- **Accessories that will make a statement to show personality and pop (light fixtures, hidden pantries, fireplaces)**

  Alfano: Hoods will be the new statement lighting element over islands but with innovative ventilation for clean air in homes.

  Rush: I think more contrast in the kitchen between the old and new, such as a designer, midcentury modern table with patina in a super polished contemporary design.

- **Other kitchen functions**

  Alfano: That is happening now—dog stations incorporated into cabinetry. Composting as well as recyclers.

  Rush: Maybe bringing [the] laundry back into the kitchen and having the right flooring underneath to handle moisture. It's popular in small European kitchens.

- **How might existing products be used in different ways?**

  Barney: Sinks can be multipurpose; appliance technology packages can be personalized to save time; and sleek designs are likely to continue to top wish lists.

Above This 210 Design House project deliberately plays with contrast in selecting dark ash wood so the ice-white-lacquered, high-gloss cabinetry does not visually merge with the white walls.

▶ **How high tech should/could we go and not risk harming the planet?**

Alfano: Technology has increased our use of energy and concern for waste and the carbon footprint. Tech companies as well as consumers all have to do their part in recycling and waste management so they don't harm our planet.

Rush: With all this technology, we have to be mindful and ask ourselves: Is what I'm consuming going to benefit the planet and me in the long run? If I add more luxury and buy a nicer appliance and it lasts 30 years versus run of the mill that will maybe die out in five years, that's being sustainable and environmentally sound. Right now, I'm sitting in an 80-year-old chair and am very comfortable.

▶ **Any ways to cut costs in designing the kitchen of the future?**

Alfano: I think modular kitchen architecture will bolster creativity and cut costs on cabinetry. The kitchen will no longer be built into the walls; instead, a metal framework could connect cabinetry within it. This flexibility offers the ability to bring a kitchen along to your next home. You don't have to start from scratch.

Rush: There's not much difference in costs to go with smart appliances. They learn how you live and that is key to being a better system for your money. Do you want to turn on the air conditioning? Say 'yes' and the air is cool fifteen minutes later. This is all about leveraging machine learning and the future role that AI will play in most of our lives. Homes that are energy efficient and high-tech ironically use fewer resources, which means lower costs overall.

▶ **Most futuristic/outlandish or over-the-top concepts you think will be done in kitchens that you've heard about?**
Alfano: My father Dr Robert Alfano is a physicist who specializes in lasers. He has patented the 'optical food spoiler,' light technology that can detect bacteria in food and tell you that it is not fresh. I have introduced this patent to a top refrigeration company to discuss the possibility of incorporating this technology into refrigerators of the future.
Barney: I see many 'futuristic' concepts being implemented in the near future, many of which we are already starting to see today: Wi-Fi-enabled sensors, automatic shut-off options, hazard detectors, hands-free fixtures and voice-activated solutions to name a few. Soon, I predict that many of these features will be seen as necessities rather than luxuries.

▶ **Do you think most of the population in 10 years might have some of these high-tech features?**
Alfano: I think ages thirty-five to fifty-five will really incorporate these tech features even though voice command appliances would be brilliant for people aging in place. The fear of troubleshooting will prevent the elderly generation from embracing high-tech features.
Rush: It will become the norm as tech changes and comes down in price. Fifteen years ago, we didn't have smartphones in our pockets.

▶ **Any red flags to be aware of? Is it difficult to fix broken tech items?**
Alfano: It will be a necessity for companies to have longer warranties and troubleshooting experts on hand to help fix issues.
Rush: With smarter appliances and complicated systems, they are sometimes easier to diagnose and tell you what's wrong with them. As far as red flags: make sure the contractor you use is comfortable with products you're using and that they don't cause any security or privacy issues.

▶ **With everything in the kitchen done for us, what is left for us to do?**
Alfano: Time is precious. With more time on our hands, we will be able to sit down at the table with our families and friends and really enjoy a meal and greet the day.
Rush: We can focus on making a better society when we have more free time. It's happened in the past. There's intellectual enlightenment as soon as our basic needs are taken care of, allowing for a higher level of thinking and caring.

CHAPTER 9

Auxiliary Spaces

Homes consist of main rooms such as the kitchen, dining room, living room, and bedrooms. Those may be the most important, but they gain necessary support from the auxiliary spaces. These additional rooms or areas may be found either adjacent to or within a main space, such as a kitchen. They play a supporting role in the kitchen achieving its full potential. In relation to the kitchen, notable auxiliary spaces include a storage room and wine cellar, a pantry, a laundry, separate mud room for accessories and day-to-day items (which can also function as a crafts room), and a butler's pantry or separate workspace for extra cooking and cleanup.

As with any new space, think about how to carry through colors, styles, and lighting from other rooms to maintain cohesion. Almost anything can work with proper thought and planning. Here are some of the many possible auxiliary spaces to consider, either within your primary kitchen or as an extension of the kitchen workspace, depending on square footage and budget.

A separate laundry room was one of the first extensions from the kitchen. Sometimes it was brought upstairs in a multistory home, with a laundry chute installed. Then it got an overhaul to become a more glamorous, less utilitarian area, often with a door leading outside. However, a laundry room was always designed to function well with space for equipment, a sink (which is also good for gardening), shelves or closed cabinets for detergents, baskets for dirty and clean washing, an ironing board, and a place to fold and sort.

The most practical flooring can withstand wetness. Patricia Gaylor, an interior designer based in Las Vegas, Nevada, likes to use Marmoleum, a type of linoleum made from natural, hypoallergenic materials. In larger homes, it is common to install two laundry rooms or have equipment dedicated for towels, quilts, and other big items, says architect Bob Zuber, AIA, partner at Morgante Wilson Architects. Some also place the laundry room near bedrooms, either on the main floor or upstairs.

Decades ago, **a mud room**—often known in England as a boot room—became a space literally to shed muddy shoes and dirt upon entering a house from the outside. In recent years, a mud room has often included a door from the outside that was used more than the front door, particularly if the house lacked a garage. It also has become known by some as the "drop zone," says Gaylor, where, upon returning home, everyone drops their belongings—coats, hats, boots, books, lunchboxes, keys, and more.

Opposite Custom cabinets in this mud room designed by Claire Staszak, Centered by Design, allow for maximum storage with minimal space. At only 14 inches deep, these lockers are great for hanging backpacks and other sports gear.

Page 184 The goal of this mud room designed by Malka Helft, Think Chic Interiors, was to bring the outdoors in with a happy whimsical feel with F. Schumacher & Co.'s Balloons wallpaper.

Page 185 (clockwise from top left) Susan Brunstrum, Studio Brunstrum, uses navy blue laundry/mud room cabinetry in the same color as the kitchen island for continuity of design; Brunstrum includes efficient storage and cubbies in the multipurpose space; In another house designed by Studio Brunstrum, the laundry room was placed upstairs near the bedrooms, with the mud room downstairs off the garage.

Good features of a mud room include built-ins; individual cubbies or lockers for each family member to stash stuff; a large closet for sports equipment; a pet spa, and a feeding station if the household includes animals—sometimes with a pet door to the outside. It's not uncommon for a mud room to be combined with a laundry if the house has limited space. Again, durable flooring is key, and a fan/exhaust is a must if the room is used by pets or is humid. As more expense is given to these spaces, they've become more attractive with handsome tiles, lively colors, and nice personalizing features.

Coffee centers took off when companies like Miele and Nespresso debuted handsome coffee and espresso machines and milk frothers to make quality java at home. This led to a need for storage for all the pods, tea bags, sweeteners, mugs, spoons, stirrers, and other utensils. Zuber recommends this area be on the periphery of a kitchen, away from the main work triangle, where everyone can help themselves without impacting kitchen traffic. If there's no room in the kitchen, this coffee area can also work well in a separate butler's or walk-in pantry, alongside other small appliances.

"Walk-off" or washable mats help to clean shoes of mud or debris from outside before entering the home. For good organization, interior designer Patricia Gaylor recommends having ample hooks in cubbies or on walls, so spaces don't become a jumble. If you own pets, have a hook for pet leashes, too. Another idea is a docking station to charge devices. If more space is available, consider a half bathroom (with a toilet and a basin), which doesn't have to be as fancy as a front-of-the-house powder room might be.

Page 186 Synergy Design & Construction combines the mud room and laundry into one large space and adds a full-sized kitchen sink and faucet to create a multifunctional space that makes cleanup a breeze.

Page 187 A stunning coffee station with bold paint, walnut finishes, and Dolce Vita Quartzite counter organizes mugs, spoons, sugar, coffee beans, and a grinder. Designed by Nancy Jacobson, Kitchen Design Partners, and Elizabeth Scott Design Group

Opposite Designers Tiffany Mansfield and Lisa O'Neil, Mansfield + O'Neil Interior Design, San Francisco Bay, California, provide additional storage in this butler's pantry and workspace to keep the main kitchen clutter free. Architecture by Fergus Garber Architects

Above (left) Jean Liu of Jean Liu Design attractively displays wine storage in a handy location; **(right)** Clad in Farrow & Ball's deep green hue called Monkey Puzzle, this hidden bar, also designed by Jean Liu, is loaded with personality and functionality.

At-home bars today are typically located upstairs near a kitchen or even in a living space. Many emerged during the pandemic as homeowners mixed their cocktails and mocktails at home rather than venturing out to restaurants and bars with trepidation. Practical designs feature closed and open storage for liquor and glassware, a dishwasher, small sink, an ice bucket, napkins, and other utensils, maybe a refrigerated drawer, beverage center or wine cooler, and mirrored, painted, or wallpapered back walls to make the area dazzle. Zuber likes to put a bar off a family room where the main entertainment takes place, though sometimes it works best on the lower level. "It's really the equivalent of a mini kitchen," he says.

Wine storage allows wine to be properly stored in a temperature-controlled cellar on racks and in refrigerators, but those without the quantity of bottles to make it a worthwhile investment may be happy with a small wine refrigerator or open racks in a corner of the kitchen, away from heat and sunlight. In 2022 one manufacturer, Dometic, debuted a five-bottle DrawBar cooler, which resembles a drawer and has a solid or glass front.

Super pantries have emerged since homeowners began wanting multiples of equipment and more counter space but didn't want all the work and messiness on view in their main kitchen work area. Some people use these back pantries to heat up food. Zuber's firm recently designed one for a family with four boys who like to prepare snacks on their own, and the parents are delighted not to see the mess in the main kitchen. Others use them as a catering kitchen for entertainment where lots of prep work takes place. The best-equipped ones include a refrigerator, sink, dishwasher, beverage center, microwave or cooktop, some pots and pans, and open and closed storage. When space and budgets permit, these may rival the size of many homeowners' primary workspaces.

GRAPE EXPECTATIONS:
DESIGNING A CUSTOMIZED WINE CELLAR

In conversation with Monica Lewis, MCR, CMKBD, UDCP,
with J.S. Brown & Co. designers in Columbus, Ohio

If you're a wine aficionado, your collection might be growing and require more than a simple wine rack poised on a kitchen counter or in a dining room or a wine fridge on the floor. Maybe it's time to consider a customized wine room that offers lots of storage in a temperature-controlled environment. Having one is a great way to entertain and put your personal stamp on a fun, interesting hobby. You can set a budget for the amount you spend on the room and the bottles—and how you store them. Here are some tips:

- **Location:** I prefer the basement. It has mechanical advantages that make it easier for a contractor to deal with the necessities. A basement tends to stay at a more constant and controlled temperature than elsewhere in your home. Also, in the basement, the wine is protected from light and there is generally less vibration than upstairs on a bouncy wood-framed floor. Some contractors will use the space under basement stairs and add interior sliding glass doors to create a cellar. It's a good use of space and less expensive than building a new wine room.

- **Design:** It does not have to reflect the architecture of the house. This is a niche space in the home much like a powder room, kid's bathroom, or a basement bar. It's for fun, entertaining, and short-term use. Also, it's closed off and may not be visible.

- **Shelves/racks:** Wine racks are traditionally seen in wood (red wood predominantly, which absorbs moisture but is not sustainable). Lately, I've seen some really cool metal rack systems—stainless steel and iron—using cups and pins that stick out from the wall. It creates a sleek, clean floating effect. Some people use less expensive wood and then high-end cherry and walnut, depending on the price point.

- **Humidity-controlled, cooling device:** If in a basement, it depends on how many bottles the owner stores and how much the owner wants to invest. Some clients will invest in a couple of small wine fridges for their favorite wines that they want to keep cooler, such as sparkling and white wines.

- **Personalization:** I did a cellar that has materials in the space that really spoke to the homeowners, such as interesting ceiling tiles and a circular halo light fixture. Another way to add personality is a beautiful dump and rinse sink with fabulous faucet for rinsing out glasses and serving dishes if you drink wine there and eat.

- **Windows:** Natural light can generate heat that can damage wine. If there are windows nearby, use black-out shades that you draw down when not in use and up when friends and family come to visit.

- **Lighting:** LEDs, with a warmer than normal Kelvin temperature, add pizzazz, come in colors, and don't give off heat. There is no need for task lighting in a wine cellar. In a cellar I designed, the LEDs are built into a vanity rail—one that tilts up and displays labels. Overall lighting should be something that gives a nice soft glow for ambiance and enough light to see the labels and what you pull down from your shelves.

Pages 190–191 A dim, outdated, and understated living room was transformed by Lori Gilder, Interior Makeovers Inc., into an open-plan, engaging, contemporary home bar and lounge.

Page 192 Not only is a wine cellar functional, but it also offers a glamorous backdrop. Designed by Jean Liu, Jean Liu Design

Opposite A kitchen desk helps with management of household paperwork in this kitchen designed by Susan Brunstrum, Studio Brunstrum.

Above Synergy Design & Construction turns a barely used formal dining room into an oversized butler's pantry with ample overflow storage and space for food and drinks prep when entertaining.

Following pages Nicole Ellis Semple, AIA, and Scott Rappe, AIA, Semple + Rappe Architects, anchor the corner of a large open living space with a built-in desk, offering a quiet nook for working.

Work nooks help those who may not have another space for work or like to be close to the center of action yet are bothered by the sight and sound of people clanging pots and pans, talking, playing music, and watching TV. What's happened of late is that some have "closed up" part of an open-plan layout with a little nook near or off the kitchen for this purpose, possibly with a pocket or other door to shut out sounds. But it can also be located in a corner, just as Nicole Ellis Semple, AIA, and principal architect at Semple + Rappe Architects in Chicago, Illinois, did in one Chicago home. There are also excellent white noise machines that can drown out unwanted sounds.

Lower-level rec room secondary kitchens are back in vogue since to construct one by remodeling is less costly than adding on square footage upstairs. Appealing features of a lower-level kitchen include a source of natural light through large window wells or a walk-out area; a high enough ceiling—at least eight feet, but nine feet is better—that might require digging down (also pricey) since ductwork may take up some of the height; a comfortable stairway to descend; a history of no water or, if there was a problem, it's been corrected with a sump pump and French drains, and a floor that won't get mildewed if it gets wet. (Even dry basements have gotten wet lately due to climate changes.) Before proceeding, be sure to ask the family: Will they regularly venture downstairs and use it? Some will say yes, but won't, particularly young children who don't want to be away from their parents. Many teenagers will relish a private retreat, however.

CHAPTER 10

Outdoor Kitchens

Cook, gather, and eat. Imagine a kitchen in your own back yard on a terrace, patio, or deck for an impromptu cookout or cocktail party. You might have a simple barbecue unit hooked up to a gas line or a propane tank or a more elaborate, built-in showcase with all the equipment and elements you're accustomed to inside, including running water.

You might throw some steaks on the barbecue unit's grill. Or, if you've extended your outdoor kitchen to include a fancier set-up that includes a high-end grill, refrigerator, sink, kegerator, pizza oven, counters, and storage, there's less need to run back between inside and outside. Just relax and soak up some fresh air and wonderful garden aromas, sights, and light. In the evening, you might savor a glorious sunset.

Nature's greenery is known to benefit physical and emotional well-being—which is why more hospitals are adding gardens for their patients, staff, and visitors to enjoy. During the Covid pandemic, being outdoors became a boon for those concerned about poor indoor air quality and germs. That made the outdoor kitchen matter more than ever. Today, back-yard kitchens are proliferating, coast to coast and in the Heartland, too.

However, as much as you may want an outdoor kitchen and have the money in your budget, it may not make sense to go overboard. The first rule of thumb is to predict how much you'll use it. In the cold Northeast and Midwest, come winter you can don a hat, coat, gloves, and even boots, but it's not as much fun. In the warm Southern and Southwestern states, year-round outdoor cooking may be a daily event, but extremely hot come summer. Think about how you'll entertain outdoors so you can decide which equipment, tables, chairs, and umbrellas you may need, and determine your budget. Many who installed elaborate and expensive outdoor kitchens have found they don't use all the bells and whistles as much as expected.

Keep the following in mind when planning your dream outdoor kitchen.

PLACEMENT

Locating your outdoor kitchen near a door to your indoor kitchen makes sense. This reduces the number of steps in and out for bringing utensils back and forth—unless you have all you need outside at your fingertips. A newer trend

Opposite A custom outdoor kitchen, designed by Bilotta Kitchen & Home, is perfect for pouring drinks and snacking poolside.

is arranging an outdoor kitchen area near a larger window that can open and work as a pass-through to an indoor kitchen. Be sure the area is large enough. Landscape designer Michael Glassman of Michael Glassman & Associates, Sacramento, California, says his clients often underestimate the amount of space they'll need for equipment, as well as the table, chairs, and umbrella. In fact, landscape architect Marc Nissim, owner of Harmony Design Group, Westfield, New Jersey, suggests planning an outdoor kitchen and dining area to be 20 percent larger than expected for good traffic flow and so people can pull chairs out comfortably.

SETTING

If you have a choice of areas, also consider the view you want to savor while cooking—and dining. Sometimes, the kitchen will be part of a larger entertainment zone with comfortable seating, even a water feature of a pond or swimming pool. Good materials for a floor include bluestone, pavers, tile, travertine, concrete, teak, and faux wood. Best to keep the choice contiguous with other hardscape materials in your yard for a cohesive look and what's easiest to clean from messy cooking and eating spills, Glassman suggests.

GRILL

"If you have natural gas in your house, connect the grill to that," says Nissim. You also may want an electric line since many grills have lights and some other appliances like a warming drawer or refrigerator that require electricity to run. If you can't do a gas line, get a propane tank and have it attached. Make sure you fill it regularly. There are also charcoal grills, kamado-style ones that use charcoal and smoke food, and pellet grills that use wood.

The barbecue unit you choose will depend on how you like to cook, how you want your food to taste, and how many guests you plan to feed, because the size of grills varies greatly. "A good basic model usually measures 36 inches to 52 inches," Nissim says. Position the barbecue close, but not too close, to your kitchen door. It's best to check your local building codes for regulations since there are concerns about fire and wood or vinyl materials on houses and nearby. Some units include side burners to heat items such as baked beans and garlic bread or to boil fresh corn and seafood. And if you want to prepare a rotisserie chicken, you'll need a model that offers that attachment. "But don't go overboard," Glassman advises. Few people use all the extra fancy equipment.

REFRIGERATOR

If you don't want to keep running between your inside and outside kitchens, it's wise to add a refrigerator. There are models designed specifically to withstand colder temperatures and sit underneath a counter. The most traditional size measures 34 inches tall and 24 inches wide and deep. If you prefer a smaller model, consider a refrigerator drawer that can also be built in. Serious beer aficionados may want a kegerator for beer on tap.

SINK

Having a sink requires extra planning if you want hot and cold water since it will need to be connected to your sewer line and winterized with antifreeze. "In the Northeast, it gets complicated," Nissim says. In worst cases, it might not be used that much for cleaning dishes and glasses but could offer a place to serve as a big ice bucket or present some seafood on ice for guests.

PIZZA OVEN

It sounds great to be able to grill your own at home, and some companies like Kalamazoo and Alfresco make sophisticated models that work by natural gas and fire up the heat to replicate the taste and texture of a wood commercial design for pizza pies. These sit on a countertop. Not surprisingly, these models are expensive. Even pricier is building a freestanding masonry or stone fireplace and having a pizza oven incorporated. Think $25,000 or more. Glassman and his wife prepare great pizza on their barbecue with a pizza steel. "We do so every Friday night and make the dough and sauce. It's restaurant quality," he says. Ooni Koda also manufactures a 12-inch, gas-powered pizza oven that's a few hundred dollars and can sit on a countertop.

Above Drawing inspiration from the architectural era of the house and exotic journeys travelers took, the Adeeni Design Group commissioned bespoke Moroccan brass lanterns to illuminate the counters of the stone pizza oven. The space is also adorned with elegant blue and white Chinese pottery.

Following pages Nestled in the bustling heart of downtown Denver, Colorado, this mission-inspired custom home and landscape conjure an enchanting and cozy atmosphere with old-world charm, designed by Abby Rupsa, principal landscape designer/owner, Botanical Living.

TRASH CENTER

It's so easy to forget to include trash cans but so useful to make room for one. Few people want to lug the indoor trash cans outside for each meal, especially for large gatherings. Keep rubbish bins concealed if you can by tucking them under a counter, suggests Nissim. And be sure there's a sturdy cover so animals of all kinds do not help themselves to your leftovers.

BUILT-IN DESIGNS

If you're having more than a freestanding barbecue or grill, it's worth considering built-in components in a storage unit to gain counter and storage space in the form of drawers or cabinets. The look is neat and keeps all of your accessories together. Most often, the structure is built from stones or brick with a facing of stone, brick, or wood.

A good countertop that will withstand the cold is granite. Nissim favors a leather textured style, which doesn't require staining. Glassman also likes poured concrete but says it requires staining and sealing. He advises avoiding synthetic materials that may separate in the heat. For this feature, he suggests going longer than expected—at least eight feet and with three or four feet or so for counters on either side of a grill to cook and later to serve. He also prefers arranging the counters in an L or U shape so the cook can face diners rather than have their back to guests. And he likes to leave a hole in the counter and insert a metal sleeve to install an umbrella to shield from heat and rain or even snow! Nearby, he may have a separate bar with cantilevered edge with stools for sitting and/or a pergola or other open-air structure where diners can sit and be partially protected. These types of features should be left either fully or partially open above so air can circulate and keep smoke out.

LIGHTING

Lighting is key for night-time use, preferably with LED bulbs, which last longer, are more energy efficient, and can be programmed automatically. You may also want to add colorful bistro-style or rope lights for a festive, party mood, even if it's just one or two people enjoying food prepared and eaten outdoors!

HEAT

If there's a structure overhead like a pergola, you can hang radiant heating bars. Drop them down like a pendant. Or you can do an outdoor radiant floor if you have tile or porcelain.

FAN

"Some homeowners also find a fan useful to keep air circulating, which also can help with bug control," says Glassman. They are guests who are not welcome!

MELDING OUTDOOR & INDOOR KITCHENS
FOR A FAMILY THAT LOVES TO COOK & ENTERTAIN

In conversation with Michael and Elaine, Sacramento, California

Michael Glassman and his wife Elaine moved into a new home in 2019 and promptly designed their indoor and outdoor kitchens from the outside in, a novel approach.

The goal was to make the two spaces function and flow seamlessly as one, with all the accoutrements of two upscale, well-equipped, and comfortable kitchens. Michael and Elaine love to entertain, and they host a special Halloween party each fall.

Michael followed his own instincts with the design, which involved having the outdoor kitchen as close as possible to the indoor one. "This makes preparing food and barbecuing for outdoor or indoor entertaining and dining efficient," he says. He also had the outdoor kitchen and dining area level with the floor of the indoors to make carrying trays back and forth safe and easy.

Now, after a long day, the two can cook on the grill, unwind, sip wine, dine, and enjoy the fresh air to the fullest alongside those who matter most.

To maximize on functionality and design, Michael and Elaine:

► placed the outdoor kitchen directly behind the indoor kitchen, through a set of big sliding doors that flow out to the outdoor dining table;

► tore out the aggregate patio that required a step down out of the sliding doors and raised it to be level with the indoor floor;

► covered the entire outdoor patio in silver travertine tile, making the space feel more expansive;

► added an oversized countertop, covered with Blue Dunes granite, to complement the silver travertine tile;

- installed a shaded overhead structure with energy-efficient fans and Dark Sky LED lighting in the outdoor dining space, bar, and serving area for cooling and insect control—while the fan and lights are within reach of the cooking area, this area was left uncovered so the smoke from the barbecue can easily escape;

- built the outdoor kitchen in an L-shape from a concrete block, facing it with horizontal strips of tiger wood to match the posts of the overhead shade structure, which satisfied the desire for ample cooking and serving space;

- installed a 36-inch Blaze stainless-steel grill, warming drawer by Fire Magic, and plenty of stainless-steel storage drawers and cabinets for platters and utensils; and

- designed a bar at the kitchen island, which allows guests to participate in food preparation and conversation while Michael and Elaine cook.

Budget: $35,000

Timeline: One month; however, it was part of a larger house remodel and garden redo that included the pool. They removed and redid everything around the pool but kept the shape.

Professionals involved: RC Haseltine Construction

Biggest challenge: "Living in the house while [the] remodeling was [being] done," Michael says.

Best feature: "Our indoor and outdoor kitchens are perfect for entertainment," Michael says. "The flow between the two and their dining areas allows our family and friends to cook together in the same spaces. The kitchens make cooking as much a part of entertaining as serving and eating. They create a space for community and a cohesive look."

Regrets: None

CHAPTER 11

In Conversation with the Pros: Five Design FAQs

Whether designing a kitchen from scratch or remodeling an existing one, it's a complicated and deeply personal process. Asking questions helps us to define and communicate what is important to each of us and how to progress. Remember the adage: there are no stupid questions—especially when it's your time and money. There is no single answer to most questions; instead, settling on the most realistic options is more than half the battle.

Of course, you may drown in all the available choices, which is why it's important to do your homework—look, study, read reviews (take some with a grain of salt), ask questions, touch, and take materials home, if possible, to see how they perform. Here are some suggestions:

- ▶ Pour lemon juice or red wine on a slab of quartzite or marble and see what happens to the material. That way you're forewarned about potential stains and scratches. Do you view them as signs of loving labor or an eyesore you'll find hard to live with?
- ▶ Tape possible paint colors in large samples to a wall and look at them during the day and at night. (Keep in mind that paint colors may look a bit different than the samples, and the tone can change depending on other colors in the room.)
- ▶ Put different LED bulbs in your lighting fixtures and ceiling cans to see what color temperature you like for different uses—tasks, mood making, and overall general lighting. Test out some of the newer LED bulbs that change color with the right app on your device.

We asked four experts—Linda Reiner, Jodi Swartz, Suzan Wemlinger, and Kristi Will—five questions that represent several that are frequently asked today. These types of conversations bring home the message that you should take any expert's input as a starting point and add your own spin when selecting your design choices. In the end, consider heeding this advice from Swartz: "I know people who are good cooks and can cook on any appliance. I know people who don't cook and have the most expensive appliances they rarely use. But you, the homeowner, need to be the ultimate decider," she says.

Opposite A collaboration between designer Tom Vecchio, Bilotta Kitchen & Home, and Patrick J. Hamilton, Patrick James Hamilton Designs, made this light-filled kitchen much more efficient and integrated into the rest of the home.

- **What are your thoughts on open shelving that can take away valuable storage?**

  Reiner: If you're replacing a cabinet with open shelving, most homeowners then add a pantry-type cabinet elsewhere to supplement the missing storage space.

  Swartz: Yes, there are lots more kitchens with this style and many shelves are not just wood but metal, which adds a glamorous touch. The advantages are that they add a modern sensibility, allow in more light to a room since they don't block as much space, and often cost half the price. For anyone with memory challenges, having items on view helps them. Also, no knobs eliminate the problem of arthritic hands that have trouble with a turning motion.

  Wemlinger: One has to consider storage when making the decision to replace cabinetry with shelves, so a small galley kitchen may not be the best type of kitchen to edit out storage space.

  Will: When designed correctly, open shelving can create more storage than closed cabinetry alone. For example, if your kitchen has an odd-sized nook where closed cabinetry won't work, open shelves can be customized to fit those dimensions. Or, if you have an awkward corner, you can install L-shaped open shelves. A combination of closed cabinetry and open shelving can offer the best of both worlds, allowing you to use more spaces in a stylish, practical way.

- **What's most prudent to reuse from an existing kitchen to save on costs? Any benchmarks on the age of appliances or cabinets?**

  Reiner: To save money (and to be sustainable), many homeowners keep their existing cabinet boxes and reface them by having an experienced installer remove doors and drawers, laminate the boxes with a veneer in the new color choice, and install brand new doors and drawers. The cost can be up to a 50 percent savings over replacing with new boxes. When it comes to appliances, all refrigerators keep food cold, all stoves and ranges cook, and all dishwashers clean. The difference is often the bells and whistles they feature, which are sometimes the first things to break and need replacing. Same goes for flooring and countertops. One key is to make any appliance look newer by integrating it for a built-in look, even if it's not a fully integrated model. Some can be partially done with matching cabinet panels that simulate the refaced kitchen cabinets.

  Swartz: I recommend to clients that they reuse appliances or a faucet if they can as long as they still work and are the right size. It's also more sustainable. An exception is when something is ten years old and starts to need repairs, it may then be time to replace it. If they want to plan for larger sizes, we design for that 'next' appliance (like a larger refrigerator or range) by adding in design elements that may be removed, when new items are purchased, and ready to be installed.

  Wemlinger: During the height of Covid and even now, it's sometimes wise to keep what you have because of the supply chain delays, which have gone on for months/years and are still occurring periodically with certain items. Cabinets may need replacing if boxes or shelves sag or

Make sure that any open shelves are secured well into the walls and not loaded down with too many things. Heavy objects can cause shelving to sag.

When appliance repairs start adding up in dollars and time, it may be more economical to invest in new equipment.

Opposite In this kitchen designed by Morgante Wilson Architects, wood and steel open shelving contributes to the eclectic, industrial-inspired aesthetic of the space and showcases colorful serving ware pieces, while also allowing natural light to flood through from the windows behind.

Opposite The quartzite slab adds beauty, durability, and functionality with a honed leather texture, color variation, and dramatic movement in the design. Designed by Lori Gilder, Interior Makeovers Inc.

Above Timeless tiles from Island Stone collections, from left to right: Plain Ash White and Just White Gloss from the Nomad collection; the Tule Matte-colored subway tile from the Glass Essentials collection; shimmering monochromatic ripples of glass mosaic Elongated Hex tiles in Oceana Matte, also from the Glass Essentials collection.

show significant wear, but if the original cabinets are solid and high quality, they can be professionally painted (usually sprayed, and the doors and drawer fronts are sprayed off-site). New cabinet hardware and soft-close hinges are an easy switch, so now the kitchen both looks and functions better than previously.

▶ **How can the backsplash add style yet remain affordable?**

Reiner: A backsplash is important since if walls are painted or papered, they may get dirty from cooking and water spraying. This is why a tile or other hard material that's easy to clean makes sense for durability. What's hard is that the sky's the limit in choices. You can go with a classic subway tile laid in a traditional rectangular format or something a bit edgier such as a hexagonal pattern or one with texture. Years ago, many people went with glass tiles in narrow width but those already have waned in popularity.

Swartz: It is jewelry for the room, and I tell clients that they can 'play' with the backsplash, as well as hardware. When you get sick of either, change them out, as neither need be expensive. Better to keep the cabinetry and countertops 'saleable' when remodeling.

Wemlinger: Backsplashes did seem like an afterthought, didn't they? To me, a tile backsplash can make a statement and really bring the fun part of a kitchen renovation—the pretty stuff—together. I've never been a fan of the four-inch backsplash that is the same material as the countertop. To me it looks clunky and, truthfully, basic-builder grade. Likewise, adding a tile backsplash above an existing four-inch stone backsplash is equally irritating: it's essentially two backsplashes and looks redundant. No matter how nice the materials are, it just looks like an afterthought. Selecting a tile for the backsplash should be a part of the design in the beginning stages of selection of materials.

Opposite Durable and
affordable quartz covers
the perimeter of the
countertops and island
in a kitchen designed
by Rebecca Pogonitz,
GOGO Design Group, and
Nancy Jacobson, Kitchen
Design Partners, who sought
a minimalist yet warm look.

► **A white kitchen can help resale. But what if we want to do something a bit different?**

Reiner: I suggest going to a tile store and using a color, texture, or pattern on the backsplash, which is the least expensive area to replace if you tire of it. There are also plenty of laminates now in colors and patterns that look like stone and are affordable for countertops, as well as backsplashes. Some designers are suggesting Corian®, an old favorite, because you can route it to look like tile in subway designs, squares, and diamonds, extending the countertop vertically for a designer look.

Swartz: I agree that there are so many options. You can have some painted cabinetry on an island so it's not the entire kitchen or a color in a backsplash or paint on walls, which is easy to switch. We often design by keeping the upper cabinetry white or light and adding darker, more 'family friendly' cabinetry on the base cabinetry. White cabinets on the bottom can be perishable. Lighter upper cabinetry also brings the eye up and makes the ceiling look taller. You can also add personality with your choice of the countertop. You can go for a material with veining running through it in a color, or a dark color that adds an accent.

Wemlinger: Yes, white is still going strong, isn't it? There are a couple [of] different things we can do to change the look and make it unique. One that is common (but still works, in my opinion) is to paint the island a different color or have the island in both a different wood species than the perimeter of the kitchen and a stain rather than a paint. What is ultimately selected will be based not only on personal style preferences but the other rooms of the home that are adjacent to the kitchen.

Will: There are many ways to inject personality. The trick is knowing where and why. You can get creative when selecting the color, patterns, and textures in furnishings (barstools, tables, chairs) since these will stay with you if you move. Your selection of lighting fixtures is another opportunity as you can swap these out if needed. Items that are trickier to change are surface materials like backsplashes, tiles, and flooring. These stay with the house and will be costly to update down the road.

► **How do you keep a newly remodeled kitchen from looking dated, considering ever-emerging technology and trends?**

Reiner: Choosing neutral colors and styles helps a kitchen remain timeless. For instance, years ago, homeowners chose elaborate styles. Now, subtle detail is the safest such as flat panels, those neutral colors, and subtle patterns that won't be outdated down the road.

Swartz: Back to the backsplash where you can add the bling. Or focus on hardware since it's not a huge expense to replace it. Interesting light housing can serve a similar purpose. New paint colors and combinations can do the trick too or you can always go back to white or neutrals, which never go out of style. Do research and look at kitchens from the 1940s all the way up to today. You will still see certain themes running through classic-looking kitchen spaces of any era.

> Introducing a couple of materials is certainly more bespoke than the all-white kitchen.

> Don't get hung up on the fashion of the day. Use quality materials and keep it 'quiet,' which means either modern or traditional classics that are well balanced.

Opposite Streamlined fixtures and a built-in bookshelf together make a small space more efficient and less cluttered. Natural oak flooring and white glass tiles reinforce a minimalist aesthetic in this kitchen designed by Sarah Barnard, Sarah Barnard Design.

Above Pendant lighting acts as the jewelry in this kitchen designed by Mansfield + O'Neil Interior Design. The scheme is punctuated by a pop of color in the island seating and a textured tile backsplash for visual interest. Architecture by Fergus Garber Architects

Wemlinger: Stick to some classic elements. Shaker doors on cabinets will probably not be out of style anytime soon (unlike the clunky arched door styles of the last fifty years). They are clean, simple, and work with a lot of different styles of homes. To mix things up but stay classic, a 'skinny Shaker-style' door gives a modern vibe to a classic Shaker-style door. It's the same simple look, but the stiles and rails are modified, and often only three-quarter inch wide compared to a standard Shaker door stile and rail, which is anywhere between two-and-a-quarter inches and three-and-a-half inches wide.

Another idea is to select different hardware for the island cabinets than what is used on the main cabinets. Should the hardware start to look dated, it's an easy fix. Staying away from big-ticket items that are too trendy is the key. Trends can be introduced in small doses, but keep the pricier parts of the renovation classic, and true to the style of the home. Lighting can be more on trend, as that can be changed if styles change down the road. Plus, modern lighting can really be pieces of art and keep the kitchen from looking like everyone else's. Don't be so afraid of trends that you play it safe to the point of boring. Cool modern light fixtures can make such a statement! Spend the time to research those (maybe hire a lighting designer) and select light fixtures that are, in essence, a work of art.

And stay away from the four-inch backsplash, if at all possible, as I feel this immediately dates a space. Look for a tile backsplash that is interesting in texture or shape, but not too 'out there' in color. Tile is also another fairly easy thing to change out. A little more labor intensive than some of the other suggestions, but it certainly can be done.

CHAPTER 12

Budget Remodels & Facelifts

After purchasing a new home with a kitchen that needs work, you may panic. Your funds to remodel are limited. But cosmetic tweaks can make the room look and work better for you without unraveling your cash flow.

Perfect kitchens tend to live in our dreams. Most need work or may not appeal to our taste. Walking into some might take you back in time and remind you of your grandmother's house or your parents' house—and not in the best of ways. Yet, it could be in good condition and still be sufficient for cooking, bringing in takeout food, and entertaining. A simple, inexpensive redo might be your best strategy.

To do this, we might all take a cue from Julia Child. Child's Cambridge, Massachusetts 20-by-14-foot kitchen, designed by her husband Paul in 1961, is on display at the National Museum of American History at the Smithsonian Institution in Washington, DC. It exudes dated charm and features original green cabinets, a big gas range, wooden countertops, and a serious cook's line-up of pots and pans on walls. Even with its old wooden table at the center of the room—no fancy built-in island—many adore it because it oozed charm and patina and belonged to Julia, who needs no last name. This is the place where she cooked and shared her love of food with friends, family, and (eventually) millions of readers and TV viewers. Magic happened there. She often referred to her kitchen as the center and heart of her house.

It's interesting to note that when Julia became a TV cooking star for the last three of her 1990s shows, her producers didn't overhaul the room completely. Instead, they made tweaks by removing a table, chairs, and back wall of cabinets, adding curtains, and installing a central cooking island, according to the National Museum. The room still wasn't likely in the running for any best-looking or well-organized design awards. Yet, it won our hearts because it reflected her personal imprint.

The point is this: rather than an expensive overhaul, spend money on the parts of the room that give you greatest joy. Replace what doesn't work functionally or aesthetically within reason and set a budget to change out parts that make you cringe each time you step into the room. This is about a kitchen touch-up; a way to achieve more of your personal vision reasonably and inexpensively, especially before putting your home on the market.

Opposite Hand-forged by skilled artisans, Ashley Norton's hammered hardware in satin brass features hammer marks for a rustic, relaxed feel. The texture offers designers and homeowners more of a custom look and adds a touch of luxury in any kitchen. The new hammered style is available for an array of Ashley Norton hardware and available in all the company's available finishes.

PARTIAL REDO

Jennifer Ames, broker at Engel & Völkers in Chicago, Illinois, suggests focusing first on high-impact changes such as painting or refacing fronts of cabinets and changing out hardware. Or replace a few appliances that are about to give out completely. There's only one problem. If you replace one appliance, the remaining ones may look worse—that multiplier effect. Heed this: some manufacturers offer a discounted bundle of key appliances like refrigerator, dishwasher, range, and cooktop, which includes removal of your old ones. You needn't wait for that one prominent, pricey refrigerator or range.

For a more expensive home, you may need to spend more in the kitchen to keep up with the neighbors, Ames says. "If neighbors are using all GE appliances, you needn't go with those more expensive brands (such as Sub-Zero, Wolf, Viking, Traulsen, and Liebherr), to cite a few," she says. Familiarize yourself with what's available and sustainable because there may be rebates and tax credits. Walk through an appliance showroom, go to a kitchen shop, and study websites that rate and compare equipment. Come armed with questions about what matters to most buyers. Not everybody wants equipment with apps to order groceries when the refrigerator signals it's low on this or that or be able to turn on the range while they drive home from work.

WHAT TO REDO BEFORE YOU LIST & SELL

You may not be quite ready to list your house but think about how much longer you plan to live there before selling. Life throws curveballs that we can't anticipate. Use a time plan for a benchmark—for example, five years. Make a list of all your house improvement priorities, develop a yearly budget, and set up a timeframe. Do improvements in stages: in year one, perhaps replace an appliance or two; in year two, after you've saved for longer, replace the countertops or the backsplashes; in year three, why not repaint! After five years, changes are for you rather than for resale. Then, take the plunge and add joy!

As part of your homework, enlist the advice of a real estate practitioner who knows your market well. You might also ask a designer in your area who stays up to date on local rather than just national trends. Housing markets have become much more localized.

What might appeal—or not—in an affluent New York suburb versus a small town in Iowa may be vastly different. Yes, homeowners in each area may subscribe to the same websites such as Houzz and Remodelista and shelter magazines like *Better Homes & Gardens* and *Architectural Digest*. You will see how popular white countertops and backsplashes continue to be. But that doesn't mean every potential buyer who walks in your door in Atlanta expects or wants everything white, white, white. The salesperson can advise what's trending in your neighborhood, the price range, and your demographic. Millennials have very different likes and wants from boomers; for example, they are more concerned with sustainability and technology and their tastes veer more towards midcentury modern and minimalism.

Take advice with a grain of salt. If people are switching to induction cooktops, you might consider that factor if you replace your cooktop. One appliance isn't likely to make or break a sale, so you could start with something less expensive to replace, such as dated-looking hardware. "Go with something much more modern in a newer finish that will make a big difference visually," says Suzan Wemlinger. Ask about the pecking order of what seems to matter most but also what visually looks bad, then factor in the price. You could also go in the opposite direction and first replace the thing(s) in the worst condition that might deter a buyer instantly, even if it's pricey like cabinets. Another idea is to dazzle with one fabulous item such as a new, deep, stainless-steel or ceramic sink with a long-necked faucet in a different finish like brass—now back in vogue. All choices give different returns on investment.

CONSIDERATIONS TO HELP GUIDE YOU

Quality wins out

Always invest in quality but shop around and read consumer report publications to find good-value products. You may not need a Sub-Zero refrigerator with the bottom-mount freezer that starts at almost $8,500; you could install a functional GE refrigerator for a fraction of the price at $1,500.

Know all the pros and cons of your choice. For example, painting cabinets can offer a big impact on quality, but only if they're in good shape. "If poorly constructed and not solid, warping or having the veneer separate ... paint will be the equivalent of lipstick on a pig," Wemlinger says.

Be warned that non-wood cabinets require more primers to adhere, so be sure to involve an expert in your decision. Refacing, while a good solution, won't work if doors look very dated or if cabinets are stained. "They have to be painted," Wemlinger says. And the right painter needs to be hired.

Below The Dometic DrawBar, which fits into a standard 24-inch drawer, offers wine storage for up to five bottles and features a user-friendly control panel with five preset temperatures for optimal cooling and storing of reds, whites, and sparkling wines.

Beware of being too trendy but think on trend

While you don't want to go overboard and follow every trend, some are worth noting. So many people now work from home but not all houses have an extra room for that purpose, so kitchens have taken on that role. People need space for a laptop at a counter, somewhere to spread out papers, or even a built-in desk—a feature that is now making a comeback, sleeker than before.

Buyers also want storage and consider it important to have it well organized for maximum use, so a floor-to-ceiling area for a pantry-style unit is ideal. Otherwise, many inserts are available for drawers and cabinets that do wonders to organize contents and fit in more. Wander through The Container Store to see cutlery dividers, knife holders, and spice racks that can fit within.

In a kitchen, many homebuyers want a place to sit (whether it be at a table or desk), some type of island with a beverage refrigerator, and a functional plan with good traffic flow for more than one cook to work at the same time.

Tweaks can work magic

Little tweaks can go a long way. Changing out knobs in a small galley kitchen may cost less than $200 and convey the message you're up to date. Switching out all incandescent bulbs for LED bulbs might run another few hundred dollars but can provide a good payback and conserve energy. Put bulbs where they're needed most—under cabinet shelves to view contents and counters and over an eating area or island.

Painting, an inexpensive way to freshen a room, can make it look bigger and brighter, especially if yours is unique, with cute floral wallpaper or a novel color. While that ochre hue may remind you of your trip to the desert, your buyers won't care and think, "It has to go!" right away. While white may seem boring, it's still the most popular and timeless, and there are so many variations with hints of this or that hue. In fact, design editors at *Real Simple* magazine say a warm white is visually appealing to most people.

Just as she suggested in Chapter 6, color expert Amy Wax suggests painting the ceiling first. "If you have a white kitchen, imagine going with a light blue [ceiling] instead, which will create an open, airy feeling," she says. Another approach might be to paint the walls a color you love. "Whether you have wood cabinets or white cabinets, think about painting your walls a warm mocha or butterscotch color, adding warmth and personality to your space," Wax says. "It doesn't have to be a bold color. It can simply be a color to warm up the room to make a significant change." And if you're looking to make a bold and dramatic statement, Wax suggests painting walls an elegant, classic navy blue. "It's a color that is practically a neutral, for it will complement any wood or white cabinetry."

If your hardwood floor is worn, find out how difficult and expensive it is to refinish it or lay an area rug atop the worst part. "Most buyers don't look down as much as up at cabinets, hardware, and countertops," says Ames. An alternative is to install durable luxury vinyl tile (LVT) or luxury vinyl plank (LVP) over the existing floor to save money and time. But ask a flooring contractor if it's feasible and determine whether it will lay flat. If not, this trick may prove too fruitless (and costly) to undertake.

Buyers now favor quartz over granite since it has proven durability and is available in a nice range of colors. But if you have granite, don't panic unless the color is very dark, which has become less appealing, says Ames, who adds, "Ask a designer or kitchen store for help. What's worse is to spend money on something out of date."

Backsplashes have veered toward neutrals and "away from crazy patterns and colors, which once were in," Ames says. White subway tile always works, even if you consider it a cliché; what classics become over time. For a high-end look to countertops and backsplashes, marble can be a good choice, especially in small areas to limit cost. If you're worried about stains and etchings, consider your comfort quotient if marks appear and the cost of removing them. Some people like the idea of well-worn patina and signs of use.

There's a difference of opinion about how easy it is to replace a backsplash. Wemlinger offers some caveats: "If you keep a countertop that has a four-inch extension above it to protect walls a bit but want to change the backsplash, the new tile may appear more of an add-on, no matter how nice it is. You might consider removing the four-inch section, but that can be tricky and, in worst cases, require you to switch out the counter, too." An alternative solution might be to add faux grass cloth wallpaper, including one of the new peel-and-stick designs that go up fast and can survive the humidity and wetness of a kitchen.

Budgeting helps you sleep at night

Deciding how much to spend on a kitchen (or entire house) before selling is tricky, angst-producing and, of course, depends on its condition, price range, location, and local supply and demand, Ames says. "In a weak market, it should be near perfect; in a tight market, buyers will pay over full price for an ugly duckling! I would make improvements in line with your local market and don't pay so much that you need an over-market price to recoup your investment."

Personalize the pros and cons

Having more personalized décor in a home, including the kitchen, has become popular of late and sets one home apart from another. The general rule of thumb remains not to get too personal unless you plan to stay at least five years—or don't mind ruling out a portion of buyers. For example, universal design features such as lower counters can be a visual turnoff for some, but if you need them to use your kitchen easily right now, don't worry. That's something the next buyer can change when they move in.

Bigger turnoffs are offbeat colors such as purple cabinets, Wemlinger says. Instead, bring your love of that hue into your tableware, maybe a small appliance, vases, and flowers—nothing too extreme that can't easily be removed, she says.

Offer ideas that give them a head start

You can ask an architect or kitchen designer to draw up a floor plan for a new layout for a few hundred or thousand dollars, depending on detail and how many plans or elevations the professional develops. This way you will help your buyers start to imagine the transformation of your space to theirs.

CHAPTER 13

Universal Design Kitchens

Universal design is for everyone. This includes senior adults who want to age in place, multiple generations who live under one roof, any family member of any age, and people with a disability or physical limitation(s). All benefit from a kitchen design that is tailored to meet these distinct needs. Because of advancements in design, incorporating these concepts doesn't have to look institutional or minimalistic. Homeowners can make their kitchens look and be as functional and beautiful as any kitchen might be.

In design parlance, universal design (UD) is the human equalizer, a person-centered aesthetic that makes life easier and safer for everyone. The importance of UD is growing for several reasons. The vast majority of the swelling senior population wants to age in place comfortably and safely. Responses to a 2019 American Association of Retired Persons (AARP) survey revealed that three out of four adults aged 50-plus want to stay in their homes as they age for several reasons. Multiple generations want to live together under one roof—a living situation that has become more popular, particularly among certain cultures where it is a tradition. People with disabilities and limitations need equipment with features that help avoid standing, uncomfortable reaching, and not being able to see, hear, or remember.

The kitchen, one of the most used rooms in the home, should be designed for everyone's needs as much as possible. Whether you design a kitchen from scratch, do a gut renovation, or tweak your space, it is never too early to make your kitchen more accessible. Many people believe that UD is simply for the older or disabled populations, and that's typically been the case in the past.

According to statistics from the Universal Design Project in Harrisonburg, Virginia, in 2021 there were approximately 140 million housing units in the United States. More than 67 million people in the US live with a disability, and fewer than 200,000 housing units (less than 0.15 percent) were universally accessible. The main reasons for this low percentage is homeowners' concerns that incorporating universal accommodations will be expensive and jeopardize aesthetics to end up with a kitchen that looks institutional and minimalistic. Times may be changing, however.

Opposite A spice pull-out shelf is a convenient feature that offers the ease of seeing all contents without rearranging everything stored behind, installed low for accessibility. Designed by Erin Loftin Serventi, owner/designer, E.L. Designs

AESTHETICS

Erin Loftin Serventi of E.L. Designs in Watsonville, California, a certified interior designer who is universal design certified and a green building professional, says UD doesn't need to look institutional. "Depending on the features and amenities you're looking to include, they can be integrated into the design, so the placement *enhances* the overall design," she says. With cabinetry and countertops designed to match the rest of the space, it simply feels like an extension of the kitchen, she notes.

One of the most common requests Serventi receives from homeowners is the integration of a lowered countertop space that is multifunctional and meets the needs of every family member. "A countertop height of 30 inches can work as a desk space, an area of the kitchen where a family member with limited mobility can sit while participating in the preparation of meals, and an area that's easy for small children to sit and eat or be occupied while other family members prepare food/snacks," she says. Something for everyone.

Mary Jo Peterson is a retired certified kitchen/bath designer, an educator, and a certified aging in place specialist with UD expertise in Brookfield, Connecticut. In 2005, she began designing the kitchen, bathrooms, and wardrobe of the Universal Design Living Laboratory, udll.com, a home built in Columbus, Ohio, for Rosemarie Rossetti and her husband after Rosemarie suffered a serious accident that put her in a wheelchair.

This spread Rosemarie Rossetti, PhD, lives in the Universal Design Living Laboratory in Columbus, Ohio, with husband Mark Leder. The home has earned several national certifications. Designed by Rosemarie Rossetti, Mark Leder, Mary Jo Peterson, Anna Lyon, Ardra Zinkon, and Patrick Manley.

Today, Rossetti is a certified disability-owned business enterprise, certified living in place professional, and certified senior home safety specialist. She's a popular international speaker and consultant on the UD subject and author of *Universal Design Toolkit*.

She's also an accessibility consultant experienced in designing and evaluating the built environment to include accommodations and a UD expert on the Americans with Disabilities Act. In *Universal Design Toolkit*, Rossetti lists the UD features in the Universal Design Living Laboratory room by room.

WHAT UD LOOKS LIKE

Before beginning any project, designer Serventi asks her clients what they wish for the space. The focus does not need to be on people with disabilities or old age to the exclusion of others, but on improving flexibility and access for all ages.

Since the kitchen is an important space in our homes, Rossetti offers UD guidelines for its design. "An open kitchen is the best set-up," Rossetti says. "There has to be enough space to move around if in a wheelchair, for example." She prefers the open center island concept, but other layouts work just as well—even galley kitchens, if there's enough turnaround space.

Rossetti, Serventi, and Chicago designer Leslie Markman-Stern, Leslie M. Stern Design, agree that the following accommodations can become important UD choices that allow a kitchen to meet the needs of everyone in a household.

▶ Sufficient clear floor space for work and traffic flow—a five-foot radius satisfies a 360-degree turnaround for wheelchair users

▶ Circulation routes that are a minimum of 40 inches wide at kitchen entryways to allow for wheelchair or walker access

▶ Thresholds no higher than 0.5 inches—and preferably none at any doorway—to make it easy to roll a wheelchair or walker

▶ Doors, 36 inches wide, with lever handles and cabinets and drawers with D-shaped handles, which are all easier to grasp

This spread Lisa M Cini, ASID, IIDA, Mosaic Design Studio, designed this kitchen with universal design accommodations. The large open space with a movable island and height-adjustable cabinets and countertops has plenty of room for a wheelchair or walker to move around, if needed in the future.

▶ Solid flooring, without grouting, to avoid bumps or falls—porcelain tile with a high slip-resistance is also good but needs to be installed flush. Rossetti likes luxury vinyl tile (LVT) that looks like hardwood or cork. Stained concrete is a solid level floor that looks artistic but is expensive. Markman-Stern suggests unpolished flooring material to avoid glare

▶ No area rugs, to prevent snagging, trips, and falls

▶ Open, visible, and flexible pantry storage

▶ Full extension pull-out shelves and drawers in lower cabinets to avoid bending and reaching for items

▶ Single-lever faucets mounted to the rear of a low-profile sink—touchless and voice-activated faucets are high-tech options

▶ A pot filler at a cooktop to reduce steps back to the sink with heavy cookware

▶ A garbage disposal mounted at the rear of the sink—out of the way to permit knee space underneath the sink for a wheelchair. Rossetti recommends also having a push-button switch hidden under the sink rather than on the wall. The sink might have features for easier food prep and cleanup, such as a shallow basin depth, a sink cutting board, and an over-the-sink colander

▶ Countertops at a variety of common heights for all family members: 30 inches (to fit a desk chair underneath), 34 inches, 35 inches, and 40 inches. Rossetti has one counter at 34 inches for herself in the wheelchair, 35 inches for the center island, and 40 inches for her husband, who is over six feet tall

- ▶ Toe kicks, a nine-by-six-inch space at the bottom of a cabinet, so there is room for a person's foot and footrest on their wheelchair
- ▶ A waste and recycling container on a pull-out drawer in a lower cabinet
- ▶ A side-by-side refrigerator and freezer (preferably 24 inches deep) with full-extension shelves that are easier to manage and require less room to open than other types of refrigerator doors. Serventi says that refrigerator drawers are very popular as secondary options for anyone with limited mobility, often included in islands for children's snacks. You can include a set of refrigerator or freezer drawers that stack nicely one on top of the other, installed under the countertop. These even come panel ready to seamlessly blend into the cabinetry
- ▶ Side-hinged doors on an oven and microwave at counter height to make it easier to open and avoid hunching over or lifting dishes over a hot oven door. Serventi says if a microwave drawer isn't in the budget, then install a microwave in a base cabinet for easy access
- ▶ An elevated dishwasher, at least 16 inches above the floor
- ▶ Front-mounted controls on a cooktop that are easy to read and reach
- ▶ Pull-out spice racks. "Depending on the width of the pull-out, they can hold oils and vinegars, too," says Serventi
- ▶ All lighting should be on dimmers so any occupant can have the best control over lighting that improves their vision. Serventi prefers the 2700 Kelvin (K) temperature as it gives a nice soft warmth to the space.
- ▶ Electrical wall outlets at 18 inches above the floor and controls within reach, particularly for a range hood's ventilation and a garbage disposal

- ▶ Rocker light switches that are almost flat on the wall plate and rock back and forth to turn the lights on and off more smoothly than toggle switches. It should be located within easy reach of a user, and not on a back wall. A good height is between 42 inches and 48 inches off the floor for anyone in a wheelchair or small children to reach
- ▶ A whole house HVAC-fan that runs and circulates the air 24/7 with filtration, to assist homeowners with breathing issues or asthma
- ▶ A drop zone for keys and to charge phones and tablets
- ▶ "Landing areas" adjacent to appliances, Markman-Stern recommends, to safely place hot items from the cooktop, microwave, and oven, cold items from a refrigerator, and clean items from a dishwasher
- ▶ Work zones with necessary storage
- ▶ Islands designed to include secondary appliances (refrigerator drawers, a microwave and/or microwave drawer), drawers for dish storage, a swing-up mixer shelf (to store very heavy standing mixers), and maybe open shelving on sides where larger bowls or platters could be stored
- ▶ Accessible shelving. "The rule of thumb is that 50 percent of storage should be reachable from a seated position," Rossetti says
- ▶ Various countertop surfaces to suit multiple purposes. Rossetti is a fan of quartz since she finds it functional, beautiful, resistant to stains, and low maintenance. It also comes in many colors and a non-glare or low-glare matte finish works best if the owner has sight issues. Serventi agrees that quartz is a good choice and adds that it's antimicrobial because it's nonporous. A bull-nose edge offers a nice, curved detail that is less uncomfortable if you bump into it
- ▶ Appliances in an easy-to-reach position. Serventi says their location also depends on how the family enjoys cooking and what their routines are. However, she generally prefers to place a cooktop so it's accessible to the rest of the kitchen with clearance on either side to maneuver
- ▶ Contrasting colors to help users see better; all-black and all-white kitchens offer less contrast. Markman-Stern suggests that if you put in a new countertop, use a contrasting edge
- ▶ A quiet exhaust fan, which can allow people with a hearing impairment to hear emergency signals, such as a smoke alarm, or a doorbell

HOW TO DESIGN A UD KITCHEN

When a homeowner decides to incorporate UD features, Rossetti suggests bringing in an expert with UD credentials, if you can, or someone who has previously worked with older people or people with a disability. Many remodeling and design experts have taken a UD course or received certification. She also suggests adding an occupational therapist since their expertise is to adapt surroundings to help people live better and independently.

The cost

"Some UD appliances are a little more expensive than non-UD models, such as side-hinged ovens," Rossetti says. "However, if you don't put additional costs into cabinets, plumbing, or some of the appliances with all the bells and whistles, the kitchen design is more affordable and certainly worth it."

In addition, Rossetti looks at the value and safety over time, especially if you're an older person or a person with a disability. "UD enables you to stay in your home," she says.

You may also be able to take advantage of tax credits, which will defer some of your costs, if your kitchen is designed for medical reasons. Stephen Brooks CPA/PFS, CFP®, MST of SRB & Associates, LLC in Chesterfield, Missouri, lists certain tax-deductible items that pertain to a kitchen UD:

- ▶ Widened doorways at entrances or exits to your home
- ▶ Lowered or modified kitchen cabinets and equipment
- ▶ Relocated or modified electrical outlets and fixtures
- ▶ Modified hardware on doors

At the same time, Brooks says that any "reasonable" home improvement to accommodate a person with a disability who lives in the house can be treated as a medical expense and deducted on the payer's 1040 form. The best thing to do is talk to your tax person or call the IRS for specific information relating to your situation in your area.

There's still a great deal to learn about the benefits of UD to bring more homeowners on board. We are living longer—the US Census Bureau estimates that the population of those 65 and older grew by about 34 percent in the decade from 2010 to 2019, according to *AARP: The Magazine*.

The hope for the future is that misconceptions about UD will dissipate, and, over time, our kitchens will become accessible to anybody at any age, for any aesthetic, and at any price point.

CHAPTER 14

How Resale Factors Influence Kitchen Design

As a homeowner, if you undertake a remodeling (even if you plan to settle in and stay for a few years), you might think twice about your choices for resale. When it's time to sell, what if your design choices don't appeal to the next homebuyer? This has been a common dilemma for years.

What makes your kitchen feel welcoming, comfortable, and—most of all—livable for *you*, yet also appealing to the next buyer? Do you freshen up your kitchen in neutral colors with stainless-steel appliances and granite countertops that so many families on HGTV's reality shows seem to covet? Or do you choose materials, appliances, colors, and scale that reflect your own design vision because, after all, you're going to be living with it for a while? This is a tough call. The debate may ramp up if you don't plan to live there long, especially because many big improvements can take months, even up to a year, from start to finish—particularly because various delays in supplies and work staff have become more of an issue since Covid.

Many think "let's just make do." Others might proceed with making changes for their own joy but stay safe and veer toward traditional, affordable favorites from neutral colors to time-honored materials, shapes, and textures and timeless equipment in white or stainless steel, depending on price points. Then there are always a few outliers who throw caution to the wind knowing they may rule out a pool of potential buyers. They go for what's deeply personal with materials, colors, appliances, scale, and more, redefining the kitchen through their own design vision. They believe it's worth the gamble to get what they want. It is a completely individual choice, and there's no right or wrong approach.

Several factors may help you decide which choice to make. Start by taking the temperature of the housing market. Is there a lot of inventory so your home has lots of competition? If the answer is yes, this is known as a **buyer's market**. If the answer is no and there is little housing stock, then it's a **seller's market**. The latter happened during the height of the Covid pandemic, when many people fled urban markets but found little inventory in less congested suburban and rural areas. Prices escalated and many houses even sold sight unseen. At that point, who cared if a kitchen lacked an island or had black appliances, laminate countertops, or old cabinets that looked like they were installed decades ago?

Opposite Designer Marina Case selected a classic red-and-blue color palette to keep this kitchen on trend, while Gilsenan Designs Inc. chose the mirror-brick backsplash and gray-painted cabinets, which can be considered neutral.

Above For a minimalist kitchen, integrated pantry storage and subtle color accents, along with warming elements such as wood flooring and a black enamel AGA range, enhance both daily living and future resale value. Designed by Claire Campbell, Mint Home Décor

"Buyers in such times are more forgiving," says Chicago broker Jennifer Ames. All people wanted during the challenging Covid period was a roof over their heads and a lovely yard where the family could spend time outdoors.

Generally, when there are more houses on the market, buyers can be choosier because they have the luxury to be. It's useful for the homeowners selling to keep their houses and kitchens updated to vie better with the competition. This doesn't have to translate to a full-blown expensive overhaul; it may only mean replacing appliances before the existing ones are on their last legs, or improving countertops before they're so badly dinged that the marks are noticeable. Fixing or replacing gradually makes life at home so much more pleasant and spreads the expenses out over time.

One dated item in a kitchen may not distract too much and ruin that good first impression, but there are multiple examples—brown- or avocado-colored 1950s cabinets, laminate countertops from the 1980s, and worn vinyl flooring from longer ago—that could make buyers wonder "what does the rest of this house look like if the kitchen is an outdated mess?" This is known as the **multiplier effect**. Buyers may be scared off when they start calculating how much it might cost to redo the kitchen alone. What you do to remodel your kitchen and how much you spend should depend not just on the market but also on the price of your house, others in the neighborhood, and your budget.

When fixing up a kitchen for resale, make it look fresh by deciding which three features would make the best first impression. Most refrigerators have a life span of 10 to 20 years so that's a good investment.

Stick to a budget since it's too easy to make one change after another and find your costs have escalated. Or as the expression goes, according to one architect, "As long as you're changing this, change that ..." and so on.

Ames feels if you don't do at least some work, potential buyers tend to think about what it will cost them to redo the kitchen and can talk themselves out of making an offer. She says, "Unfortunately, many overestimate the price by as much as four times. So that twenty-five thousand dollar kitchen could become a one-hundred thousand dollar project in their mind ... Moreover, they're not just thinking dollars," she says. "These days, it's the aggravation of remodeling—finding the right workpeople, getting a design drawn, waiting for parts to come in, having it all installed, and so on."

You might decide to add in something that you know many homebuyers love. It could be an island if you have room, even one on wheels. Or it could be one new, highly appealing appliance or design element such as a combination steam oven and microwave or a great oversized hanging light fixture. Designer Suzan Wemlinger adds other suggestions such as beverage centers, a touchless faucet, or pot filler. Any of these features are quite popular and impressive; they may quickly attract attention and show off your efforts.

These days, it is worthwhile choosing something off the rack or on a store's floor rather than the haute couture equivalent. Even in the best of circumstances, without pandemic delays, kitchen remodels take time. With certain supply chains still backed up, some homeowners have been asked to wait a year for their windows and appliances. Some sellers try giving buyers credit to make their own choices, which may not be the solution all like.

The reality is that most buyers want to find a house with a kitchen they love that is already in great shape—and this factor may indeed help you sell your home. However, chances are that the new owners will eventually redo all or part of the kitchen to fit their own tastes and needs. In the end, we never know what a buyer will like or how things might shake out. It's not possible to predict who is likely to buy your home or any home in the future, so only you can determine how much of a risk you're willing to take, how much you want to spend, and what you want to spend it on. Your home is your castle even if your reign might be short lived!

CHAPTER 15

Second-home Kitchens: Eat, Cook, Unwind

We all need time away from our normal routines and the stress of everyday life. Many people choose to decompress in a second (or vacation) home—whether a large and lavish house with every amenity or a small, efficient dwelling.

The best vacation homes or second homes often have kitchens different from those in primary homes. But that's the point. Typically, the vacation home design permits casual living, usually with a different aesthetic than a primary home. It is often designed to need far less maintenance. "Durability in finishes is of the utmost importance to eliminate worry and ensure a relaxed environment," says interior designer Jennifer Robin. You want to pursue your favorite passions, worry less, play more. Interior designer Patricia Gaylor says, "It's all about gatherings and easy times spent with guests and not fussing over details. Keep it simple and casual, but put your style to work."

Architect Bob Zuber agrees that most of his clients' vacation homes put entertaining as their top priority. "A lot of our clients have family and friends come for long stretches—weekends, holidays, the summer—so we approach the design to be used for more people than its immediate occupants," Zuber says. What they request, he says, are big pantries, coffee bars, refrigerator drawers near a table, beverage centers, island seating, and outdoor kitchens.

However, there's another very different type of second home kitchen that's far smaller and serves a different purpose as part of an accessory dwelling unit (ADU). An ADU is often built on an owner's primary property and used as an investment to rent out to others as part of the sharing economy.

Despite differences in size and intent, the kitchen in most vacation dwellings is still the command center. Its secondary status does not diminish its importance. During the pandemic, second homes took on a different role beyond vacation haven. They became a refuge from the outside world—somewhere to feel safe and remain healthy.

There's no single vacation kitchen blueprint that works for everyone. Your first requirement in planning is to know the exact purpose of your second home. "Obviously, location and function need to be considered, but I also encourage designs that promote connectivity," says Robin. "A large built-in banquette removes the formality in a dining space and supports closer gatherings, and your dining table may double as a game table! Designing an island with stools on two or more sides encourages connectivity, too."

Opposite An antique butcher block island adds character while the handmade tile and shiplap walls bring texture to this farmhouse-inspired pool house designed by Jennifer Robin, Jennifer Robin Interiors. Architecture by Sutro Architects

Following pages In response to the clients' desire for a serene, light, and neutral space that feels warm and welcoming, Adeeni Design Group and Sutro Architects integrated practical concrete flooring with carefully curated walnut, cedar, and bronze to harmonize with natural rope and linen, achieving the desired balance of tranquility and comfort.

This spread and following pages This weekend-home kitchen, with architecture and interior design by Andrew Franz, AIA, Andrew Franz Architect, is clad in warm cypress and green ceramic tiles that blend into the foliage of the wooded backside of the house. A banquette avails itself of morning light and sunsets over the ocean, viewed through an adjacent screened porch. The banquette is also located just inside from an outdoor barbecue and prep area so one can arrive at the table from the kitchen proper or exterior.

A second factor may be how you envision cooking and entertaining. Once at a vacation house, many people focus on unwinding and not spending all their time performing chores. Cooking may provide joy, however, particularly when others are there to help. You may want more counters for multiple chefs to prep, or a big island, if feasible, for everybody to gather. You want good equipment, though perhaps not with all the bells and whistles like in your primary home, and enough electrical outlets. And in certain cases, it may be better outfitted and more glamorous than your main home kitchen. It all depends on use and budget.

Don't forget cabinets or open shelves for dishes, glasses, cutlery, and other essentials. Gaylor favors having good storage for multiple needs, including for food so it's protected against insects and rodents and won't spoil. You also want to pare back trips to the grocery store, especially if it's not nearby, because you would much prefer to be kayaking or playing pickleball. Storage is also ideal in outdoor kitchens.

Above all, secondary kitchens should conjure the idea of fun. Vacation homes are ripe for personalization! Robin says, "I encourage people to take a few design risks in their vacation homes and infuse some whimsy and unexpected design elements. Your kitchen should have at least one conversation starter." For example, you can use local materials like wood or stone that have a rustic or industrial feel; enliven the space with colors that are evocative of the setting, such as blues for water and green for farmland; or display collections such as colorful antique Seltzer bottles or souvenirs from traveling like snow globes from around the world.

Another idea is to emphasize a theme related to a vacation hobby, such as fishing, boating, tennis, or golf. And don't forget to furnish the kitchen with some comfortable squishy seating, and practical, heated, and wipeable floors to withstand the inevitable footprints that match the season. Vacation kitchens are rooms where people linger and relax.

Opposite A palette of deep greens, reclaimed wood, and copper accents was used in this wine country kitchen designed by Jennifer Robin, Jennifer Robin Interiors. A mirrored-tile backsplash provides reflective light that enhances the kitchen's indoor/outdoor connection. Architecture by Wade Design Architects

QUESTIONS TO ASK WHEN PLANNING A VACATION KITCHEN

▶ **What kind of kitchen layout will work best?**
Consider how often you use it, how many guests will typically come, its location, and the climate.

▶ **What materials will hold up well?**
If you're not there all the time or isolated, choose items that are hearty, long-lasting, and easy to fix.

▶ **How can you cater to other needs of the home as a whole?**
This dilemma is often solved by adjacent auxiliary spaces such as a laundry, mud room, pet washing and feeding station, outdoor kitchen, at-home bar, work nook, and so on.

▶ **In decorating, do you want to play off its location or have a theme?**
In the décor and color scheme, you may choose to exaggerate a beach theme, for example, if your home is on the waterfront.

VACATION KITCHEN ESSENTIALS TO STOCK

If you plan to list your home on a sharing site such as Airbnb or Vrbo, keep essentials on hand that guests may need in the kitchen during their stay. Many people stopped venturing out during the Covid pandemic, and inflation worries continue to keep them home. Guests may be more likely to cook their own meals occasionally to keep costs down and eat fairly healthily.

Check your own kitchen to make note of what you use most and provide how-to instructions or user manuals for any high-tech appliances or equipment. According to the design pros, some essentials may include:

▶ saucepans, skillets, woks, and pots (including a lobster pot if you're near a seashore);
▶ a cutting board, dishes, glasses, cutlery, and mugs;
▶ tools such as scissors, spatulas, a ricer, kitchen scales, tongs, big spoons and forks;
▶ good-quality knives and a sharpening steel;
▶ a roasting pan and other cookware, such as a colander and mixing bowls;
▶ coffee maker, milk frother, and tea kettle;
▶ toaster oven, air fryer, or both;
▶ blender, mixer—standing or hand held;
▶ working appliances, plus a grill outside;
▶ baking equipment—measuring cups and spoons, cookie sheets, muffin pans, rolling pin, and thermometer;
▶ wine and can openers and stoppers;
▶ towels, potholders, and oven mitts;
▶ various spices, cooking oils, vinegars, salt, and pepper;
▶ some canned goods, bottles of water, soda, and cleaning supplies;
▶ storage containers; and
▶ pantry space.

CHAPTER 16

The Process & Who Does What

Ready. Set. Go. You're fired up and ready to follow our blueprint to achieve the kitchen of your dreams. These last few chapters will walk you through the entire process to completion and beyond.

Some homeowners who remodel a kitchen get lucky and the process hums along as smoothly as an uninterrupted night's sleep. Other homeowners are simply hopeful that their job won't offer too many jolts, detours, and delays and will be completed in a timely, affordable way. Having a plan in place makes all the difference for a reality that falls somewhere in between and leads to the best possibilities.

Almost everyone who undertakes a kitchen improvement thinks it's worthwhile because they achieve the look and functions they wanted and stay close to their budget. The calculations are straightforward. Our kitchens continue to have a leading role in our home lives as the heart of our homes. But gaining that dream kitchen requires a detailed roadmap. It encompasses a team of professionals who take your vision as seriously as you do and expand on it by using their expertise.

You and your professionals should sign contracts to lay forth responsibilities, planned changes, an estimated timeframe, and budget, and stipulate they'll regularly keep in contact by a predetermined method—email, phone, text— and a schedule. There should be no going off on an idyllic vacation without letting you know and leaving someone else in charge.

"Having a comprehensive process in place with the right team will set you up for success," says designer Marina Case of The Red Shutters in Hudson, New York, and Martha's Vineyard, Massachusetts. She offers five planning tips to get through the process, with an easy-to-remember acronym **CITIP**:

COMMUNICATION

Conversing clearly with all team members or through the one or two who drive the process is essential. You don't want remarks coming back from your painter such as, "You didn't make clear you wanted the finish on the walls to be eggshell and the ceiling to be a lighter shade." Whether they repaint it

> Provide design boards, grids, and charts to all key people involved in the remodeling, including yourself and any subcontractors. Marina Case's firm does this and supplies a color plan for the painters; appliance and plumbing supply board for the electrician; and drawings for the cabinet suppliers. Nothing is left to chance.

may hinge on their schedule and profit margin and not how nice you are. Yes, some clients serve hot coffee and doughnuts regularly. However, it's much better if what you want and what you think you voiced is backed up by what's in a signed written contract or in an email or paper trail. No one will be as passionate about the project as you are.

INSPIRATION & VISION

Do research before you begin and know how much you want to spend to get what you want. Even if you don't consider yourself an expert in imagining your perfect kitchen, many resources can help you begin to picture and price what you might like—or how to substitute something you're dying to have with something similar and less costly. Resources (many listed in the back section of this book) include websites of designers and architects; showrooms to visit in person and view vignettes, and samples of cabinets, tiles, and faucets; appliance stores with the latest induction ranges and pot fillers; reality TV shows; print magazines; and newspaper articles.

What you find might surprise you. One recent issue of a shelter magazine had an advertisement for a built-in filtered water dispenser. Who knew that existed? The same issue highlighted the availability of modular kitchens—cabinets that come fully assembled and are ready to install to save time. Designer showhouses, routinely organized as charitable events, also showcase ideas in room vignettes. And then there are your neighbors' and friends' homes. How about that oversized blackboard or pegboard for posting family activities for the week or a menu, which you saw and liked?

Your space, style, and budget all help ground you when making choices. Unfortunately, you may need to eliminate fantasies of multiple pieces of equipment in a small space and with a tight budget or forget having only open shelving above countertops and a glass-fronted refrigerator if you're a messy cook and housekeeper. The articles are great fun to read that say "everyone" now wants the latest trends, such as an English country-style kitchen, a corner built-in upholstered banquette so it resembles your neighborhood diner, or bold colors to offset years of white, gray, and beige. However, ask yourself if you might get tired of any of these features in a year.

TEAM MEMBERS

Select professionals with a proven track record. Having a team that has performed this type of work, day in and day out, yields a great sense of comfort. But beware if you hand everything over to one contractor. When you have a medical problem, you go to a specialist. Same with your kitchen. You may want certain specialists added for particular requests.

Maybe, hire a professional kitchen designer who will bring you samples and explain everything to you, navigate the process, and be the liaison between you and **the general contractor** (GC) and their tradespeople. If you want a sustainable or universally designed kitchen, it might behoove you to bring in a consultant who is certified in these fields. When selecting countertops and

> Marina Case's firm uses Pinterest and Houzz boards and collaborates with homeowners pulling images together until a clear vision emerges. "This is required homework as part of the teamwork and probably one of the most important steps in the process," Case says.

> Good teamwork gets the job done. Case says, "When we lead the project in combination with the contractor and kitchen designer, we are able to yield the best results."

backsplashes, the new durable Dekton material (from Cosentino) requires a special expertise to cut and install it. If you hope to salvage your existing cabinets by refinishing or refacing the fronts, find out who's available to do so and if they're worth the expense. Then ask if your designer, architect, or contractor agrees.

INSPECTIONS

Stay on top of what's happening. Take snaps with your phone and do videos in real time for documentation of each step along the way. If while a countertop is being installed it takes a chunk out of your freshly painted wall, for example, you have proof the wall was fine before the counter's installation. It's the evidence you may need to have the damage mended at no cost to you. Accidents happen and most materials can be repaired.

PATIENCE

Be flexible. In certain cases, it might be necessary to switch to Plan B when Plan A presents wrinkles. Being prepared and calm will save angst on everyone's part, and sometimes finances. Unless the process means switching out some knobs or bulbs or replacing an appliance or two, most kitchen overhauls require time—and lots of it. In fact, some cabinet manufacturers stipulated a wait of three or four months for delivery during the pandemic. At other times, there also may be delays for different reasons. In any case, demolition of an existing kitchen should not start until close to the arrival of the equipment and cabinets you ordered. You might be able to store things in your basement or garage, or your contractor may be able to store items in their warehouse, if they have one, or somewhere off-site on your behalf, and hopefully for no or little charge.

THE TEAM

This is no time to go at it alone—unless the changes are minimal, like switching out incandescent bulbs for LED bulbs or changing preferred drawer knobs. But even light bulbs offer a challenge if dimming is desired.

The first professional to hire is the person who's going to design the kitchen. This could be an independent **kitchen or interior designer**, **an architect** or both, one on staff at a kitchen design company, or one employed by a big-box store since many now offer expertise, cabinets, appliances, installation, and more. They all have the ability to look at the big picture, and envision the space and how it might be redesigned to meet your functional, aesthetic, and financial needs. They can determine if it makes sense to add on or make other structural changes, and they know—or will bring in someone who does—if you can knock out a wall to open up the kitchen or expand it. If it's a load-bearing wall, it might have to remain or, if removed, it must be done properly by professionals and may be costly. "It's key to have someone to lead the project, who also will collaborate with the necessary trades—a good traffic cop," Case says.

Checking on a project regularly is key to success. Marina Case's firm does this as part of its work for a kitchen package and finds early on what needs to be tweaked. She advises her clients promptly about when the work will be done and communicates again once finished.

Case's firm advises clients to order what they need far ahead, in case of delays, and preferably what's available. "There are plenty of great choices in good taste and doing this saves everyone so much aggravation in waiting sometimes months on end," she says.

In some cases, you might need a **structural engineer** to decide whether walls can come down or if beams or floors need reinforcing. The lead person may hire other experts, such as a surveyor, to check that anything added isn't too close to your property line if you haven't had a recent survey prepared. Additionally, you'll need someone to execute the design, the GC, who might measure the existing space and study the plan to order the right cabinets, countertops, backsplash tiles, appliances, and cans of paint, or farm out some of these responsibilities to specialist subs. However, they should still oversee coordination of all the roles. The contractor manages the flow of the work by subs and oversees the construction process.

Many contractors employ subs full-time at their company while others contract out work regularly to those who handle demolition, plumbing, electrical work, HVAC, flooring, painting, and other tasks. In either case, having a team that's used to working together helps ensure a win–win situation and avoid conflicts.

FINDING THE RIGHT TEAM

Ask the right questions and you're more likely to find the right people, especially if you've never remodeled any part of your house before. Not only do you want skilled and experienced professionals, but you also need people who really understand how you and your family members want to use the space, keep you in the loop if materials are delayed or damaged upon arrival, show up when they say they will, and clean up after themselves.

Signing a detailed contract that spells everything out is essential to a strong working relationship. You may want to have an attorney eyeball the contract too. Yes, that adds expense, but it can make a difference and mean fewer headaches and expenses later on.

Some tradespeople are better at smaller jobs and others only take whole-house renovations. Get references and see at least three or four examples of their work, if possible. Read reviews about them on Yelp and other online sources, but also trust your gut rather than solely relying on their reputation, accreditations, and recommendations.

Here is a list of questions, with input from Marina Case, to guide you in hiring your team of contractors, regardless of how you get their names. You can either ask these questions directly or ensure the responses are covered in your official documents such as the contract before signing on the dotted line. The answers to some of these questions could help you determine whether the person will be the best fit for you and your project.

▶ **How long have you been in business?**
There's no single answer but at least several years' experience with developing solutions and facing challenges should provide you with a good level of comfort.

▶ **Does your experience match what I want done?**
Don't get caught up in their statements of what they want to do; instead, listen to what they have already handled.

- **Can you provide any references or direct me to recent reviews? Can you show me any previous work you've completed?**
  See their work in person to make sure it's their work and not someone else's. Ask about styles. If all the pictures on their website look traditional and you want a contemporary design, ask if that's their preference or if they are versatile. Ideas they share should indicate their capabilities.

- **How do you keep abreast of new trends and materials?**
  It may be reassuring to know if they read shelter magazines; watch HGTV; notice social media posts by designers and architects; check out stores that sell home-related products and materials; keep their eyes open when they travel; and pay attention to paint manufacturers that debut new colors annually.

- **Have you previously worked with high-tech items and hands-free technology?**
  If you're veering towards installing hands-free faucets, for example, inquiring about their past experience can determine whether they are able to install certain items safely and securely, and teach you how to use them. Also, they should check to see if you have an adequate power supply for these items.

- **What's your view on using marble?**
  Some cabinet and countertop companies require a signed waiver if marble is your material of choice.

- **Have you earned any certifications or received any awards/recognition for previous projects?**
  Certifications matter more for some professions—architects, landscape architects, landscape designers—than for others. (See the end of this chapter.) It may satisfy your curiosity to know some have gone that extra mile or been recognized for a notable achievement in their industry. What matters most is their creativity, technique, and their finished projects. Seeing a portfolio and working in person are key.

- **Do you carry adequate liability and worker's compensation insurance, and does this apply to subs who work on my project?**
  Accidents and mistakes happen and can be costly, so it's better to be prepared and protected.

- **Do you offer an initial consultation and is it free?**
  Thoughts vary about the value of providing one free consultation, but the key is to know in advance. This is the time to spell out your needs and visions and to see if there's good chemistry. For this reason, it helps if a homeowner has compiled images of projects they like and any special requests they have, such as enough space for two sets of dishes, toe kicks on bottom cabinets, and hidden trash bins for recycling.

- **How do you charge for your work?**
  This might be an hourly rate or a certain percentage of the total fee.

- **What percentage do I have to pay upfront as a retainer?**
  Many designers require 100 percent upfront, so be prepared to pay in full. Some will want half or even a third, and it is rarely refundable. They don't want to give away their intellectual property for free.

- **What if I want to make changes to the plan?**
  Some companies may only permit a certain number of revisions along the way. Ensure they also stipulate at what point(s) in the process revisions are accepted.

- **Is there a minimum expenditure required?**
  Ask what you get for this sum if there is one. A tweak involving painted cabinets and choosing tiles for a new backsplash may not be worth their time, so have an idea of what you can afford.

- **Is my budget realistic?**
  It's prudent to have an idea of the costs before you meet. Research in advance what you think you may want to spend on appliances, tiles, and other choices. Doing so gives you some understanding that a Sub-Zero refrigerator will cost much more than a more generic brand that you can find at a big-box store. Same goes for handcrafted ceramic tiles versus those in plain white from the local hardware store.

- **Can you provide a line-item estimate of all the costs for my project? Can you provide updates if prices escalate, due to shortages and other reasons? Are you able to offer less expensive alternatives?**
  Line-item estimates can help you to see what each individual item is going to cost before you proceed. Everyone should provide updates regarding price increases, if applicable, as they occur.

- **How often will you bill for payments? How do you feel about a holdback for the punch list or until all work is completed satisfactorily?**
  Some bill monthly or every six months. It is common to withhold some funds, 10 percent or so, until all the work has been completed. Knowing their opinion on this can be beneficial in advance so it's not misunderstood as an aggressive tactic.

- **Who secures and pays for necessary permits; for example, if I live in a historic neighborhood?**
  You may know whether or not you live in a historic neighborhood, for example. Communicate this with your team and they will secure the permits, pay, and then bill you down the track for that cost.

- **What is the timeline for my project? How often are your timelines achieved?**
  Timetables vary widely depending on the scope of the project and how the contractor works, but kitchens may easily take six months to a year. Knowing whether a contractor often achieves their timeline can indicate how effectively they plan.

- **When will demolition begin?**
  This could happen when the contract is signed or after everything is ordered and received.

- **Who confirms work times?**
  This is more relevant if you live in a condo or cooperative apartment. Some buildings don't permit work before or after a certain hour or on weekends. Similarly, some buildings require a refundable deposit to be made; so find out which party is responsible for that deposit.

- **Where will all the materials be stored?**
  Materials can be in a contractor's warehouse, in your own house, or in a supplier's showroom.

- **Who hauls away old cabinets, countertops, and debris, and how often is this done?**
  Some contractors sell or donate materials to charitable organizations to reuse. Find out who gets the tax deduction in that situation.

- **Can you check the warranties for the new equipment and appliances?**
  Some warranties are connected to the company that makes the equipment and often are only for a one- or two-year period. Some materials have longer warranties. And some are only applicable under certain conditions. If the contractor has to return for a change you want but didn't stipulate in the beginning, be prepared to pay.

- **How will you protect the surrounding areas of my house during the work?**
  Some companies seal rooms off well with plastic or in other ways to keep dust and dirt spreading.

- **Will my kitchen be functional during the project? And, if not, what scenario do you suggest?**
  This can allow you to plan ahead and prepare for a particular situation. For example, the kitchen work may make living at home inconvenient so you might consider living offsite temporarily, or setting up a small, functional kitchen space somewhere else in your home.

- **Is it possible for you to bring in a porta potty to use on the premises instead of accessing my own facilities?**
  Many contractors will organize this independently. On the other hand, if you have a basement bathroom you rarely use, you can offer to let work staff use that.

- **How will we stay in touch?**
  Again, another important question to ask and decide about—but often complicated matters should be done through email and simpler issues in an email or text thread. Some homeowners may prefer a weekly call so questions can also be easily asked. Come up with a plan.

▶ **Are you available to focus on my project and meet the deadline? Will you have any other projects on at the same time?**
If they don't have a slot for you, consider whether you are willing to wait for an opening in their schedule. If not, might they recommend someone else just as competent?

▶ **How much of the day to day will you tell me about?**
This may depend on your preference. Be upfront about how much you want to know. For example, do you want to be informed if the lead person needs to step away and be advised on how long it may take? Do you want to know if other workers can quickly step in?

▶ **What if something emerges as a surprise, such as a load-bearing wall, which requires the plans to be revised? Are there costs involved in delays of this nature?**
Sometimes surprises occur, so be prepared, but usually this occurs at the beginning of a gut job when walls or ceilings or floors are opened. Delays may happen and costs may increase.

▶ **If there's an emergency, what is your expected response time?**
Most professionals try to respond to big emergencies in 24 hours. Clearly communicate with your workers about what constitutes an emergency.

▶ **Can I buy appliances and materials myself?**
Sometimes it's recommended that you go through a particular designer, architect, or cabinet company that is affiliated with your contractor. Discuss whether you have access to certain recommended professionals.

▶ **Can you share resources with us or offer any trade discounts?**
It can be so valuable knowing your hire's favorite stone yard for countertop slabs and backsplashes; preferred appliance store with top-quality products and staff to answer questions about gas or induction; and favorite cabinet retailer where you can see and touch multiple door fronts and insides, knobs, and hinges.

▶ **Will you also check on progress if you aren't working daily at the site?**
Some work requires regular inspection, such as an intricate tile installation, and regular check-ins may give you peace of mind.

▶ **Is there a process for resolving disputes?**
Some companies have an escape clause in their contract if there are numerous problems that can't be resolved. The contract may stipulate professional mediation first, for example.

▶ **Do you understand my vision?**
You can tell a lot after you've talked about your wants and needs and your design criteria by their questions, comments, and initial plan.

ACCREDITATIONS

Accreditations can set members of your team apart and may help you decide who to hire; however, many other factors go into your choice, including their recent work results, pricing, and rapport you have with them.

- **LEED.** The Green Building Certification Inc. (www.gbci.org) administers the certification to reflect knowledge about green building and sustainability, an increasingly important trend to conserve resources.

- **LEED AP.** This indicates even more knowledge. Some areas of the United States have specific programs such as the Southeast's EarthCraft to indicate good building practices related to energy, water, and climate.

- **Architect, AIA.** The American Institute of Architects (www.aia.org) offers its AIA designation to those who are experienced and have been in good standing for at least 10 years. Nominees have also completed 10 cumulative years as an AIA member prior to the nomination deadline. Many architects attain LEED or LEED AP status in addition to indicate interest in green building and sustainability practices. "It's important but sometimes a challenge for architects to convince clients that a sustainable project is worth the extra costs," says John Kirk, AIA, an architect who works on many such projects for his firm, Cooper Robertson, New York City, New York.

- Some architects have earned the additional distinction of FAIA, which means that the American Institute of Architects has made them a fellow and bestowed this recognition on them for their career achievements.

- **Kitchen designer.** The National Kitchen & Bath Association (www.nkba.org) offers different accreditations such as Certified Kitchen & Bath Professional (CKBP) and Certified Kitchen Designer (CKD).

- **Certified remodeler.** The National Association of the Remodeling Industry (www.nari.org) also offers different levels of specialty from Master Certified Remodeler (MCR) to Certified Remodeler Project Manager (CRPM).

- **Certified graduate remodeler.** The Remodelers' Council of the National Association of Home Builders (www.nahb.org) lists CGR contractors on its site. They have been trained in business practices helpful to the remodeling industry.

- **Interior designer, ASID.** The American Society of Interior Designers (www.asid.org) offers its ASID designation for those who have extra training and have passed the organization's exams. The group's NCIDQ certificate is another level to indicate more skills and coursework. The group also offers specialization such as its AAHID, from the American Academy of Healthcare Interior Designers.

- **Landscape architect, ASLA.** The American Society of Landscape Architects (www.asla.org) trains and certifies architects to work in the outside environment and design for different purposes, from functionality and conservation of the environment to emotional and physical health through healing and meditation, and also aesthetics.

- **Landscape designer.** Landscape designers who may belong to the Association of Professional Landscape Designers (www.apld.org) do work similarly to their architect counterparts, with some exceptions. "They cannot take on commercial, industrial, or federal design work," says landscape designer Michael Glassman, founder of Sacramento, California-based Michael Glassman & Associates. Their training is generally shorter than what architects go through.

CHAPTER 17

Teamwork: All Together Now

Assemble the right team members for your job from the start and you lessen your chance of experiencing hurdles, angst, and an unreasonable budget and timeline. Like an orchestra, which brings many musicians who play different instruments together to make one lovely sound, it takes many members of a kitchen team to create one beautiful space that reflects personal taste, functional needs, and the desired budget.

A kitchen has so many moving parts—appliances, cabinetry, different types of materials, and wiring—that completing work becomes an intricate process. How do you pull this all together to fashion one harmonious, finished room? It demands attention to details, an expert overseeing all the steps, following the right order, and bringing in other specialists as needed.

You, the homeowner, are the ultimate decider. You're the one who will live in the kitchen and home. You have the final say to determine who assumes all the vital roles to get the job done, what the budget will be, what will go into the job in terms of parts, and what won't.

You need to feel confident in your choices and listen to your experts' ideas, but at the same time, you need to voice your thoughts clearly throughout the process so there's no disappointment at any point and certainly not at the end. This is no time to play second chair.

What does all of this entail? We provide some steps to help you stay on the right path. Remember that every kitchen job is different depending on the scope of its work and the team hired, as detailed in Chapter 16. Sometimes unexpected bumps occur, but you'll be able to get back on track because your extra planning accounts for unpredictable occurrences.

MEET FOR A CONSULTATION

After interviewing several potential designers or architects and asking them the questions listed in the previous chapter, you are ready to begin. At this point, your designated project leader should know your preferred style and color palette, how you want to work in your future kitchen, any specific needs you may have, and what you can spend.

You've also shared your best-case-scenario timeline (with built-in wiggle room to account for supply chain delays, worker illness, and surprise finds, like a rotted subfloor that needs to be replaced).

The consultation is the time to fine-tune all your ideas and share them with the designer or architect so they can start to draw up your plans. If you want to keep certain features—cabinets or appliances—let them know. They may have already shown you rough sketches and price estimates.

Most kitchen designs live in our dreams. Now is the propitious time to be brutally honest with yourself about how your dream kitchen can become a reality. Think about whether this will be a good working relationship; do we have that magic ingredient called chemistry? If you respect the contractor's creativity and judgment, they listen to you and respond respectfully, and nobody gets defensive or critical, then you have the makings of a good partnership.

Time to hit go. If not, kindly speak up and see if you can come to a meeting of the minds or bow out tactfully. Depending on the contract you signed, you may have incurred charges for design time.

PUT DOWN A DEPOSIT OR RETAINER

Remodeling a kitchen is no different from other home improvement projects with one exception: It may involve more tasks, people, money, and time. Because of the scope of the design work and number of parts involved—materials for backsplash, flooring, countertops, cabinets, hardware, appliances, light fixtures, and more—almost every designer and architect will specify a cost for the design process and charge you a deposit or retainer's fee. Ask for specifics. "The majority of cabinet companies ask for at least 50 percent, and appliances will require the full 100 percent payment," says Marina Case.

What about the costs for revisions to the plan? Most professionals allow for several revisions before the actual work begins but ask in advance how many changes are allowed before extra fees are applied. You don't want surprises. Once choices are finalized, additional change orders may dictate further charges. It's wise to have all this in a written contract.

MEASURE THE ROOM

This is a critical step to ensure new cabinets, countertops, flooring, and appliances will fit together like pieces of a jigsaw puzzle. Someone on your design team—designer, architect, cabinet company—or someone else knowledgeable will measure the entire room, including doorways, height of the room, windows, and adjoining spaces so everything will perfectly align once completed.

Your professional will also note imperfections, such as slanting floors, which require compensation, and location of outlets and recessed light cans. They will check the home's electrical circuit to be sure it can handle new equipment and that the wiring is still in good condition and up to code. If you plan to keep any existing equipment, they will measure that, too, so everything fits with the new cabinetry. To cover all bases, they will examine existing conditions by possibly taking up some flooring to see the state of the subfloor beneath.

Decide how much you want to be involved in the process and let all parties know. Be brutally honest, based on your schedule and personality. If you're a micromanager and like to watch every nail hammered, share that in advance. This may even keep your team on its toes. If you envision going on a Caribbean vacation and returning when all is done, share that, too! Will you have a proxy in your absence—someone else coming in to check on the progress and quality of work? It could be a smart idea.

Ask your design professional to take notes at meetings or when on-site and send you summary notes that detail all that transpired. (You may also want to take notes or record your sessions to keep everyone on the same page but ask permission first before you record.) "Having this knowledge before you're too far along can be a game changer to be sure both homeowner and designer are on the same page," Case says.

It's important to have the cabinet company do their own measurements. Case says, "The company the homeowner orders cabinets from is responsible for the final measurements, so everything fits properly, including appliances." However, when she takes on a kitchen job, she is the one who specifies—with input from the homeowner and the cabinet company—the choices of color, finish, style, handles, interior compartments, and other detailing.

Outside conditions also matter if an addition is being installed, and a survey may need to be ordered to see if the allowance near the property line is sufficient. Same goes for a house in a historic district with certain indentures, if a window, door, or roofline can be altered, and if you need to apply for a variance in your town or village.

TACKLE ALL THE CHOICES HEAD-ON

At the same time your designer or architect is working on your plan, they'll also compile a list of components you'll need, including appliances. You'll either shop on your own or with them or others for specific choices. Ask them if they charge for time spent shopping together; this, too, should be in the contract and at a flat rate or hourly fee.

Be thorough to save time and money and get accurate bids for all components and labor. Also, decide if you want a sustainable kitchen or sustainable options, universal design, or a smart kitchen. The list below may help ensure that nothing has been left out of the planning process.

- ▶ Cabinetry—material, finish, color, knob(s), and specialized inserts, including in-drawer outlets that become docking drawers or open a special way if UD
- ▶ Hardware
- ▶ Countertops—thickness and type of edge
- ▶ Backsplash—same as the countertop (called countersplash) or different and how far up the wall the material, if added, goes
- ▶ Paint or wallpaper (especially if there is no backsplash)
- ▶ Appliances—after measuring correctly, consider all possible options and decide what you like best; for example, standard or high-tech, type of range or oven, door style, and freezer location on a refrigerator
- ▶ Lighting—layers and types of bulbs, including some fixtures, light plates, and switches
- ▶ Wiring, ducting, vents, and other HVAC needs
- ▶ Flooring—and whether radiant heating will be installed underneath
- ▶ Windows
- ▶ Doors to the outside and between the kitchen and adjacent rooms
- ▶ Wider openings or thresholds for accessibility
- ▶ Full or partial walls
- ▶ Extras that personalize your kitchen, such as a pet feeding station, baking center, and themed décor

STUDY FLOOR PLANS & ELEVATION DRAWINGS

How your kitchen looks now and will look once transformed is conveyed in a two-dimensional floor plan or blueprint drawn to scale—typically one inch equals one foot. The drawing includes all critical information, such as windows, doors, cabinets, appliances, islands, table and seating, trash can, pantry, and so on. You can quickly tell how many cabinets and drawers you will have and their sizes and the extent of countertops—is there enough space to roll out

Go over each choice with your designer or architect and ask if they can accompany you or if you're on your own. Case says that most of her clients shop on their own for appliances. When it comes to paint, however, she likes to be involved and offers a paint plan that specifies colors and finishes for all surfaces—walls, ceilings, trims—to achieve a coordinated look. But each professional works differently.

Ask how everything is billed. Some professionals charge retail; others offer their trade discount without any mark-up while others may tack on a percentage for a mark-up. Periodically ask what items have arrived and what are still on their way. Case suggests clients keep a spreadsheet or other detailed written list since it's too easy to forget with so many parts.

pastry, make a cup of coffee with the milk frother nearby, and temporarily rest clean dishes after removing them from the dishwasher? You can also see if you like the amount of space between the sink and the refrigerator, for example.

These plans can be intimidating. Learn to decipher the symbols and don't be afraid to ask if there is something you don't understand or cannot visualize. Try to picture yourself in the space. Take time to study each part of the plan and compare it with what you currently have. Make a list of what you liked and didn't like in each existing zone for prepping, cooking, and cleanup.

In addition to the two-dimensional plans, your team will produce elevations using computer-aided design (CAD) software or the new Revit or Chief Architect software so you can envision the room in three dimensions. These visuals make it far easier for some to understand how the room will look, especially for those new to the process.

Your design pros will also show the exterior of your home, especially to see where any outside door leads—possibly to a deck and outdoor kitchen. You'll also want to see how that big new window you wanted looks from the outside in. A great garden would be a lovely sight when washing dishes, but a brick wall may make you reconsider that choice. In that case, a shade over the window can hide it from view.

Once you see all the plans, it may be time for another meeting or to list any changes you want before sharing them. You may have forgotten that you want a place to hang up book bags, coats, and hats when you first walk inside, if you don't have a mud room. The good news is you are getting closer. It's almost time for the plans and list of components to be given to a contractor for bids.

VISIT SHOWROOMS, STONE YARDS, & APPLIANCE STORES

This is the fun part for many—the outing to look at material choices, cabinets, and lighting. Many designers have samples in their offices or will send you or accompany you to showrooms and stone yards to look and learn. Take notes and jot down what you like and why. Take photos or record video with your smartphone in case you want to look back at your choices or share them with others. Do research, too. Does engineered quartz appeal or do you prefer more natural quartzite, and do you want to pay extra to have it bookmatched when slabs are put together? Do you want a faucet that requires only a tap or a command to turn on or does modern technology scare you? Flooring choices are also crucial since you're on your feet a long time in any kitchen.

Ask how all choices measure up for longevity. Inquire what warranties are for different appliances, whether you should buy a protection plan, and whether cabinets and countertop choices also carry protection as long as cleaning and normal wear and use are involved. Find out what normal wear and use implies rather than being satisfied with a vague description.

GET BIDS

Once the plans are approved and choices made, it's time to call in a contractor(s) and subs. If you have long worked with someone and trust their workmanship and pricing, you may be content getting only one bid. If not, consider two or three contractors to bid out work. Besides studying the plans, they'll want to visit the site to check on potential load-bearing walls, soffits and whether they can be removed, whether floors are level, and what walls may be altered, removed, or added. All of this will affect prices for demolition and installation.

At some early point, a contractor may bring in their subs such as a particular plumber, electrician, HVAC specialist, or a stone specialist to install quartz, marble, or other materials that require extra expertise. If you have subs that you want to work with, be sure they and the contractor can work together well. The cliché is true: too many chefs in the kitchen can spoil the broth.

Everybody submits numbers, and they are added up. Don't worry if the cost looks high. Simply go back to the drawing board if it exceeded your expected budget, prioritize what you want, and make some hard choices. Cut away; it's no different from looking at less pricey houses once you add up the listing price, real estate taxes, and so on. You also are wise to build in at least 10 to 15 percent more to spend, which rose in many cases to 30 percent at the height of the Covid pandemic. And many prices are still rising. The reason for the moving target in price is that some choices get discontinued, and newer ones may cost more.

> Don't just rely on your design professional for a contractor's name. Ask friends, other workmen, and kitchen-related businesses for names, too, and check reviews and references. Case puts into a contract that whoever the client chooses for contractor represents a good fit so the client can't come back and blame her for the choice later.

SIGN A CONTRACT(S)

Before you start work and finalize choices, your designer (or architect) will draw up a contract to sign that will detail who is responsible for which part of the job and itemize what the charges encompass. Typically, it should contain:

▶ how their time is compensated—a flat fee or hourly rate, what's included, and what may be on the house;

▶ what your design team is purchasing for you and if at retail or wholesale and with what kind of markup as stated earlier;

▶ how often site visits are made;

▶ how any differences or problems are resolved; and

▶ a rough timeline for the entire job.

During the Covid pandemic, it was hard to guarantee a final end date with delays of materials due to shortages or human error, but the situation has improved. A rough estimate is helpful. You also want to know how substitutions will be handled, if necessary. You're also likely to have a separate contract that should include:

▶ number of site visits;

▶ a rough estimate of daily arrival and departure times;

▶ how other rooms will be protected while work is going on; for example, if sheets of plastic will keep out dust;

▶ whether staff is permitted to use a homeowner's vacuum, bathroom, and refrigerator;

- how cleanup is managed and how often it will be done;
- what happens to big items such as old appliances and countertops that need to be disposed of;
- any materials or supplies that need to be purchased;
- which subs will be involved;
- how to resolve any differences or problems; and
- how much of the final invoice can be withheld until the punch list is fully satisfied.

The key in each case is that a contract offers more legal protection than a chat and a handshake. It works for the design pros and vendors, too. Read each contract carefully and consider having an attorney examine them. Many contractors use a standard template but will add or delete parts for your specific case.

NEAR THE FINISH LINE

Only make the final payment once the job is fully completed. Walk through the premises with your designer, architect, and contractor and see that your punch list has been totally satisfied. Take notes and photos. Typically, the punch list represents 10 percent to 20 percent of the total cost. This should be stipulated in your contract so the contractor can't complain later when you hold back $10,000, for example, until all is corrected.

HEAVE A SIGH OF RELIEF

When everything is put back in place and cleaned up, boxes unpacked, and you start to use your newly remodeled kitchen, you'll probably find that all the dust, anxiety, and concerns about costs were worthwhile. Some adjustments may be needed. A new door might have to be shaved to open and close smoothly, some knobs tightened, paint patched, and floors cleaned. Accidents happen. You may need to be taught how to clean that special quartzite countertop. This is all to be expected. Some big challenges may also occur and that's why you're glad you used a team of pros and signed a contract.

Most of all, welcome to your new kitchen! Bon appétit!

HOW TO WORK WITH A CONTRACTOR

Your designer or architect is crucial to developing a design for your kitchen (or any room), but it's the contractor and their subs who will execute it. "Pick one carefully," advises designer Sharon McCormick, Allied CT, AIA, Sharon McCormick Design in Hartford, Connecticut, who's been in business for 30-plus years. Here are her observations that will help determine whether your project will be heavenly, hellish, or somewhere in between.

▶ Make sure you have a good rapport with the contractor you hire. Clear and frequent communication is the key to a successful project, so make sure your contractor listens to and addresses your concerns. Maybe get them to repeat what you say after making a request or ask them to write it down as a clear reminder.

▶ Set boundaries at the beginning of the job and at every opportunity, rather than when something irritates you. Examples could include no one on the premises before 8:00 am, no music playing, or no foul language and smoking in your house.

▶ Clearly let the contractor know how you expect your house to look at the end of the day. If you want it broom-swept clean every day and no tools left in the middle of the room, say so.

▶ Make sure your contract specifically says no product substitutions, if this is important to you. "I specify exactly the products to be used, and I don't want the contractor to use a lesser quality one," McCormick says.

▶ Document every conversation you have and summarize it in an email to the contractor, so you have a dated written record of what was agreed upon and when. (You can also record your conversations, but ask permission first.)

▶ Ask what happens to the cost if changes are requested. Don't think the contractor is going to do extra work for free. When the scope or materials of the original contract change, make sure your contractor is up to date on change orders. If not, you'll be in for a big surprise when they present them at the end and expect to be paid.

▶ If something doesn't look right to you, address it on the spot. The further the job goes, the more expensive and difficult it becomes to fix possible errors.

▶ Treat the workers occasionally (provide drinks, lunch, or a morning snack) so they know they are appreciated. If they've done something well, tell them. Everyone loves to have their extra efforts or skills noticed. Tell the boss, too.

▶ Write a punch list of details left to complete every so often, but definitely near the end of the job before you make the final payment. It may be hard to get a contractor to come back to do little things once the big stuff is done and they've been paid.

Credits & Resources

We extend our immense gratitude to the below companies, individuals, associations, publications, and resources for their valued contributions to this book.

Featured Designers, Architects, & Industry Professionals

210 Design House (Chicago, IL)
www.210designhouse.com

Adeeni Design Group (San Francisco, CA)
www.adeenidesigngroup.com

Alexis Ring Interior Design (San Francisco, CA)
www.alexisring.com

Amy A. Alper, Architect (Sonoma, CA)
www.alperarchitect.com

Amy Wax (Montclair, NJ)
www.amywax.com

Ana Williamson Architect (Menlo Park, CA)
www.awarchitect.com

Andrew Franz Architect PLLC (New York City, NY)
www.andrewfranz.com/studio

Anna Lyon Interior Design LLC (Columbus, OH)
www.linkedin.com/in/anna-lyon-b932b230

Annie Mandelkern Interiors, LLC (Sands Point, NY)
www.anniemandelkern.com

Arcanum Architecture (San Francisco, CA)
www.arcanumarchitecture.com

Arch-Interiors Design Group, Inc. (Beverly Hills, CA)
www.archinteriors.com

Architecture Allure, Inc. (San Francisco, CA)
www.archallure.com

Arditi Design (New York City, NY)
www.arditidesign.com

Ashley Norton (Pompton Plains, NJ)
www.ashleynorton.com

Bandd/Design (Austin, TX)
www.bandddesign.com

Becker Architects (Highland Park, IL)
www.beckerarchitects.com

Bilotta Kitchen & Home (Mt. Kisco, NY, New York City, NY, and other locations)
www.bilotta.com

Bolster (New York City, NY)

Botanical Living, LLC (Northglenn, CO)
www.botanicallivingdesigns.com

Build with Ferguson (Chico, CA)
www.build.com

California Faucets (Huntington Beach, CA)
www.calfaucets.com

Carlisle Wide Plank Floors (Stoddard, NH)
www.wideplankflooring.com

Carol Kurth Architecture + Interiors (Bedford, NY)
www.carolkurtharchitects.com

Centered by Design (Chicago, IL)
www.centeredbydesign.com

CetraRuddy Architecture (New York City, NY)
www.cetraruddy.com

Christopher Peacock (Greenwich, CT)
www.peacockhome.com

Christopher Matos-Rogers, Coldwell Banker, Real Estate Agent (Atlanta, GA)
www.coldwellbankerhomes.com/ga/atlanta/agent/christopher-matos-rogers/aid_250601/

Cooper Robertson (New York City, NY)
www.cooperrobertson.com

CPI Interiors, Decorating Den Interiors (Stittsville, OT, Canada)
www.cpi.decoratingden.com

DeCleene Creative (Chicago, IL)
www.decleenecreative.com

Decorating Den Interiors (West Chester, PA)
www.decoratingden.com

Designs for Living by Wendy LLC (Key Stone Heights, FL)
www.designsforlivingvt.com

Dishington Construction/Jensen Hus Design Build (Natick, MA)
www.jensenhus.com

Dometic Group (Multiple locations)
www.dometicgroup.com

Earl B. Feiden Appliance (Kingston and Latham, NY, and other locations)
www.earlbfeiden.com

E.L. Designs (Watsonville, CA)
www.eldesignsco.com

Elizabeth Scott Design Group (Lake Forest, IL)
www.escottdesigngroup.com

Engel & Völkers (New York City, NY, and Chicago, IL)
www.evrealestate.com/company/about-us

Eric Goranson (Portland, OR)
www.aroundthehouseonline.com

Feinmann, Inc. (Lexington, MA)
www.feinmann.com

Fergus Garber Architects (Palo Alto, CA)
www.fg-arch.com

Ferguson Bath, Kitchen & Lighting Gallery (Newport News, VA, and multiple locations)
www.fergusonshowrooms.com

GI Stone (Chicago, IL)
www.gistone.com

Gilsenan Designs (Warwick, NY)
www.gilsenandesigns.com

GOGO Design Group (Skokie, IL)
www.gogodesigngroup.com

Harmony Design Group (Westfield, NJ)
www.hdglandscape.com

Home Improvements Group (Woodland, CA)
www.homeimprovementsgroup.com

House Seven Design (Indianapolis, IN)
www.housesevendesign.com

Hursthouse, Inc. (Bolingbrook, IL)
www.hursthouse.com

In Detail Interiors (Pensacola, FL)
www.indetailinterors.com

Interiors by Alison (Carlsbad, CA)
www.interiorsbyalison.com

Island Stone North America Inc. (Watsonville, CA)
www.islandstone.com

Jacob Laws Interior Design (Saint Louis, MO, and Charleston, SC)
www.jacoblaws.com

Jean Liu Design (Dallas, TX)
www.jeanliudesign.com

Jeffrey A. Eade (San Francisco, CA)
www.jaearchitect.com

Jeffrey Neve Interior Design (Walnut Creek, CA)
www.jeffreyneve.com

Jennifer Ames, broker, Engel & Völkers (Chicago, IL)
www.evprivateoffice.com/advisor/jennifer-ames

Jennifer Post Design (New York City, NY)

Jennifer Robin Interiors (San Anselmo, CA)
www.jrobininteriors.com

Jensen Architects (Calistoga, CA)
www.jensen-architects.com

Jessica Lautz (Washington, DC)
www.nar.realtor

Joseph A. Rey-Barreau (Lexington, KY)
https://design.uky.edu/people/joseph-rey-barreau

J.S. Brown & Co. (Columbus, OH)
www.jsbrowncompany.com

Katherine Shenaman Interiors (Palm Beach, FL)
www.shenaman.com

Kaufman Segal Design (Chicago, IL)
www.kaufmansegal.com

Kipnis Architecture + Planning (Evanston, IL, and Boulder, CO)
www.kipnisarch.com

Kitchen Design Partners (Northbrook, IL)
www.kitchendesignpartners.com

Kitchen Magic, Inc. (Nazareth, PA)
www.kitchenmagic.com

KitchenVisions (Natick, MA)
www.kitchenvisions.com

Kitchen World Inc. (Williamsville, NY)
www.kitchenworldinc.com

Kristi Will Interior Design (Half Moon Bay, CA)
www.kristiwilldesign.com

KTGY Architecture + Planning (Irvine, CA, and other locations)
www.ktgy.com

L'Atelier Paris (New York City, NY)
www.leatelierparis.com

Landry Design Group (Los Angeles, CA)
www.landrydesigngroup.com

Legacy Construction Northeast, Inc. (White Plains, NY)
www.legacydevelopmentllc.com

Leslie M. Stern Design, Ltd. (Chicago, IL)
www.lesliemsterndesign.com

Lori Gilder Interior Makeovers Inc. (Beverly Hills, CA)
www.lorigilder.com

Mac Renovations (Victoria, BC)
www.macreno.com

Maestri Studio (Dallas, TX)
www.maestristudio.com

Manley Architecture Group (Columbus, OH)

Mansfield + O'Neil Interior Design (San Francisco, CA)
www.mansfieldoneil.com

Marcela & Logan Architects (Encinitas, CA)
www.marcelalogan.com

MasterBrand Cabinets (Carlisle, PA)
www.masterbrand.com

Maypop Building Workshop (Nashville, TN)
www.maypopbuilds.com

Merkoh Development

Michael Glassman & Associates (Sacramento, CA)
www.michaelglassman.com

Michele Alfano Design LLC (Rockland County, NY)
www.michelealfanodesign.com

Mint Home Décor (Los Angeles, CA)
www.minthomedecor.com/about

MODTAGE design (San Francisco, CA)
www.modtagedesign.com

Molly N Switzer Designs, LLC (Portland, OR)
www.facebook.com/mollynswitzerdesignsllc

Morgante Wilson Architects (Evanston, IL)
www.morgantewilson.com

Mosaic Design Studio (Columbus, OH)
www.mosaicdesignstudio.com

nuHaus (Chicago, IL)
www.nuhaus.com

Oregon Trail Remodeling (San Marcos, CA)
www.oregontrailremodeling.com

Patricia Gaylor Interiors (Las Vegas, NV)
www.patriciagaylor.com

Patrick James Hamilton Designs (New York City, NY)
www.instagram.com/patrickjhamiltondesigns

Paul Russo Architect, PC (Locust Valley, NY)
www.russoarchitect.com

Paula Winter Design (Highland Park, IL)
www.paulawinterdesign.com

Peruri Design Company (Los Altos, CA)
www.peruridesigncompany.com

PHX Architecture (Scottsdale, AZ)
www.phxarch.com

Pressley Design & Co, Decorating Den Interiors (Benbrook, TX)
www.bonniepressley.decoratingden.com

ProSource® of Hudson Valley Wholesale (Poughkeepsie, NY)
www.prosourcewholesale.com

RC Haseltine Construction (Davis, CA)
rchaseltineconstructions.com

Rachel Laxer Interiors (London, UK, and New York City, NY)
www.rlaxerinteriors.com

Rebecca Reynolds Design (Hamden, CT)
www.rebeccareynoldsdesign.com

Rodman Paul Architects (New York City, NY)
rodmanpaul.com

Rossetti Enterprises, LLC (Columbus, OH)
www.rosemariespeaks.com

Salcito Custom Homes, Ltd. (Scottsdale, AZ)
www.salcito.com

Sarah Barnard Design (Santa Monica, CA)
www.sarahbarnard.com

Semple + Rappe Architects (Chicago, IL)
www.splusr.com

Sharon McCormick Design (Hartford, CT)
www.sharonmccormickdesign.com

Sharpe Development & Design (Bronxville, NY)
www.ashleysharpe.com

Showcase Kitchens (Manhasset, NY)
www.showcasekitchensny.com

SRB & Associates LLC (Chesterfield, MO)
www.linkedin.com/in/stephen-brooks-cpa-pfs-cfp-339b685

Stephanie Mallios, Realtor®-Salesperson, Compass (Short Hills, NJ)
www.compass.com/agents/stephanie-mallios

Stephanie Wohlner Design (Highland Park, IL)
www.swohlnerdesign.com

Studio Brunstrum (Chicago, IL)
www.studiobrunstrum.com

Studio Garrison (Portland, OR)
www.studiogarrison.com

Studio Pressman (Raleigh, NC, and Los Angeles, CA)
www.studiopressman.com

Sutro Architects (San Francisco, CA)
www.sutroarchitects.com

Suzan J Designs,
Decorating Den Interiors (Milwaukee, WI)
www.suzanw.decoratingden.com

Synergy Design & Construction (Reston, VA)
www.renovatehappy.com

Taylor Viazzo Architects (New Rochelle, NY)
www.tvarchitects.com

The Hudson Company (Pine Plains, NY,
New York City, NY, and other locations)
www.thehudsonco.com

The Red Shutters (Hudson, NY,
and Martha's Vineyard, MA)
www.theredshutters.com

The Turett Collaborative:
Architects & Interior Designers (New York City, NY)
www.turettarch.com

Think Chic Interiors LLC (White Plains, NY)
www.thinkchicinteriors.com

Unscripted Interior Design (Centennial, CO,
and Santa Ana, CA)
www.unscriptedinteriors.com

Wade Design Architects (San Anselmo, CA)
www.wade-design.com

William Caligari Interior Design (Great Barrington, MA)
www.williamcaligari.com

Zinkon Creative Studio (Pickerington, OH)
www.zinkoncreative.com

Associations, Industry Resources, & Publications

AARP: The Magazine
www.aarp.org/magazine

American Academy of Healthcare Interior Designers
www.aahid.org

American Council for an Energy-Efficient Economy
www.aceee.org

American Institute of Architects (AIA)
www.aia.org

American Lighting Association
www.alalighting.com

American Society of Interior Designers (ASID)
www.asid.org

American Society of Landscape Architects (ASLA)
www.asla.org

Association of Home Appliance Manufacturers
www.aham.org

Association of Professional Landscape Designers
www.apld.org

Bob Vila Home Improvement
www.bobvila.com

Building Green
www.buildinggreen.com

Decorative Plumbing + Hardware Association
www.dpha.net

EarthCraft
www.earthcraft.org

Energy Star
www.energystar.gov

Fellow of the American Institute of Architects (FAIA)
www.aia.org/design-excellence/college-of-fellows

Forest Stewardship Council
www.fsc.org

Green Building Advisor
www.greenbuildingadvisor.com

Green Seal
www.greenseal.org

HomeAdvisor
www.homeadvisor.com

Houzz
www.houzz.com

International Association of Lighting Designers (IALD)
www.iald.org

LEED, The Green Building Certification Inc.
www.usgbc.org/leed

LEED AP
www.usgbc.org/credentials/leed-ap

National Association of Homebuilders
www.nahb.org

National Association of REALTORS®
www.nar.realtor

National Association of the Remodeling Institute
www.nari.org

National Kitchen & Bath Association
www.NKBA.org

Passive House Institute/US (PHIUS)
www.phius.org

The Remodelers' Council of the National Association of Home Builders
www.NAHB.org

The Universal Design Project in Harrisonburg, Virginia
www.universaldesign.org

Universal Design Living Laboratory
www.udll.com

US Green Building Council
www.usgbc.org

WELL Building Standard®
standard.wellcertified.com/well

Wolfers Lighting
www.visualcomfort.com/wolfers

References

"Cost vs. Value Report 2023." Remodeling, accessed November 18 2023
https://www.remodeling.hw.net/cost-vs-value/2023.

Dr. Gernot Wagner, "Cheaper, but Expect Growing Pains," New York Times, August 12, 2022
https://www.nytimes.com/2022/08/12/opinion/environment/climate-bill-house-inflation-reduction.html

"Green Guide to Recycling Appliances and Electronics." PartSelect, February 29 2024
https://www.partselect.com/JustForFun/Guide-to-Recycling-Appliances-and-Electronics.htm

"Homeowner's Guide to the Federal Tax Credit for Solar Photovoltaics." Department of Energy, last modified April 1, 2024
https://www.energy.gov/eere/solar/homeowners-guide-federal-tax-credit-solar-photovoltaics

Isler, Robert. "NKBA Releases Its 2023 Design Trends Report." NKBA, October 19, 2022
https://nkba.org/research/nkba-releases-its-2023-design-trends-report

Lance, Ryan. "5 Takeaways from NKBA's 2024 Kitchen Design Trends Report." NKBA, October 3, 2023
https://nkba.org/research/5-takeaways-from-nkbas-2024-kitchen-design-trends-report

Stannard, Liam. "8 Innovative Smart Waste Management Technologies." BigRentz, October 15, 2021
https://www.bigrentz.com/blog/smart-waste-management

Steward, Gisela. "Appliance Recycling Near Me." Recycling Center Near Me. November 20, 2023
www.recyclingcenternear.me/recycle-appliance-near-me

Photographer Credits

Special thanks to all photographers for their expressed permission to print their images. The page references to all related images are provided below.

Acknowledgments

Like any successful remodeling project, writing a book needs a solid team. For this project, we want to acknowledge the many designers, architects, and firms we interviewed, some of them more than once; companies that guided us with best practices; the photographers who took images of the stunning kitchens; dozens of homeowners who shared their personal experiences and sometimes their budgets; our publisher and the terrific editorial and marketing staff, including Danielle Hampshire, Nicole Boehringer, and Gina Tsarouhas; and our computer guru, Tim Magnarella, who helped us with occasional tech glitches and transferring large files.

We'd like to acknowledge the herculean efforts of the marketing and public relations folks, writing experts, design professionals, and homeowners who complied graciously whenever we contacted them. Any omissions or inaccuracies are not intentional. Thank you to: Rena and Todd Abrams; Megan Annecchiarico, Sharp Think; John Algozzini, Hursthouse Inc.; Erin Baebler, Jo Communications; Mary Beth Duehr, Duehr & Associates; Brian Eskew and Matthew Frey, Dometic Group; Julia Duke & Co.; Kim Gonthier, Davis Gonthier; Elyse Goyen, Aimée Mazzenga Inc.; Erica Islas, EMI Interior Design; Jay Koziarz and Sarah Lyons, Taylor Johnson; Liz Lapin, In Detail Interiors; MasterBrand Cabinets; Anne Monaghan, Monaghan Communications; Stacey Moncrieff, National Association of REALTORS®; NKBA; Kristin Ohnmacht, Bilotta Kitchen & Home; Courtney Pisarik and Sophie Wells, Ink PR Group; Barbara Pressman, Barbara Pressman PR; Andrea and Justin Pollak; Peter Radzwillas, Radzwillas Kitchen & Bath Design; Ginny Reynolds, Blitzer & Company; Studio Shed; Cheryl Savitt, Savvy Words; Estelle and Jeff Schmones, Suzanne Epstein Sokolov, Sokolov Marketing; Lauren Stakutis, Feinmann, Inc.; Alex Abarbanel-Grossman, Karen Shan, Adam Sullivan, and Chris Sullivan, C.C. Sullivan LLC; and Peg H. Williams, APR, Public Relations Manager and Communications, Build with Ferguson.

Thank you to our family members and close friends to whom we talked incessantly about what excited us most in the world of kitchens at any given time—an in-vogue hue for a backsplash or accent wall; a new tile shape or flooring material; the latest gadget to make cooking joyful and easy; a high-tech appliance that can be operated from a smartphone; or contemporary lighting to illuminate the finished room.

It was an enormous task to gather images and blueprints of kitchen designs to reflect design current trends and practical, sustainable, and beautiful materials; appliances that harked back to elegant older styles or looked ahead to technological breakthroughs including AI; and different layouts in both small and large spaces. During our years of research, we realized that cooking and entertaining are still the driving forces behind kitchen remodels, whether indoor or outdoor, and regardless of geographic location, size of the space, and budget. Above all, the secret ingredient in any successful kitchen overhaul is personalization—it's *your* kitchen, for *you*. We learned that most homeowners care as much about this space as we do.

We are delighted to share *Kitchen Conversations* with you. We hope that you make it part of your kitchen conversations too.

Barbara and Margaret

About the Authors

Barbara Ballinger (Hudson River Valley, NY) is an award-winning journalist, author, and reporter who has interviewed a variety of celebrities and experts including Tipper Gore, Martha Stewart, Danny Meyer, Rosalynn Carter, Lorraine Bracco, Doris Kearns Goodwin, and Ruth Reichl. She has covered diverse topics such as business, design, real estate, entertainment, food, law, and personal finance. Her work has appeared in publications such as the *GlobeSt.com*, *Chicago Tribune*, *The New York Times*, *Crain's Chicago Business*, *HGTV*, *American Bar Association Journal*, *House Beautiful*, *Multifamily Executive*, *Developer*, *Realtor*, *Robb Report*, *Travel & Leisure*, *Midwest Living*, *AAA*, NAA's *Units* magazine, and more. Of the nineteen books Barbara has authored, thirteen have been with Margaret Crane—the most recent being *Suddenly Single after 50, Not Dead Yet* and *The Kitchen Bible*. She and Crane blog weekly at lifelessonsat50plus.com. Barbara has also appeared on TV and radio, including a segment about remodeling disasters on *The Oprah Winfrey Show*, and with Crane on NPR about their last book. She formerly worked for *House & Garden Guides*, part of Condé Nast, the *St. Louis Post-Dispatch* newspaper, and *Realtor® Magazine* by the National Association of REALTORS®. She earned a BA from Barnard College, Columbia University, and an MA from Hunter College, City University of New York, and started work on her MBA.

Margaret Crane (New York, NY) is a nationally known freelance writer focusing on business, food, wine, fashion, home furnishings, and real estate. She has interviewed such luminaries as Jack Buck, Virginia Johnson, Sally Quinn, Moshe Dayan, Dr Benjamin Spock, David Ben Gurion, and Tippi Hedren, among many others. Her work has appeared in a wide variety of publications, including *The Beverage Journals*, *Crain's Chicago Business*, *Family Business Magazine*, *Inc.*, *Midwest Living*, *The New York Times*, *Newsweek*, *Realtor® Magazine*, *St. Louis Business Journal*, *St. Louis Post-Dispatch*, *St. Louis Magazine*, *The Wine Spectator*, and *Your Company Magazine*. A proven author with thirteen titles to her credit, she has co-authored with Barbara Ballinger other such books as *Successful Homebuilding and Remodeling*, *The New Homeowners Handbook*, *Apartment Living*, *Not Dead Yet* and *The Kitchen Bible*. She formerly worked as a senior writer and researcher at a nonprofit fundraising organization in St. Louis, where she helped launch and maintain an award-winning website. She has also appeared on TV and radio and, with Ballinger, spoken around the country about becoming single, including on NPR and at Barnard College. In addition, she writes website content and does ghostwriting and editing for various clients. She holds a Bachelor of Journalism degree from the University of Missouri.

Published in Australia in 2024 by
The Images Publishing Group Pty Ltd
ABN 89 059 734 431

Offices
Melbourne

Waterman Business Centre
Suite 64, Level 2 UL40
1341 Dandenong Road
Chadstone, Victoria 3148
Australia
Tel: +61 3 8564 8122

New York

6 West 18th Street 4B
New York, NY 10011
United States
Tel: +1 212 645 1111

Shanghai

6F, Building C, 838 Guangji Road
Hongkou District, Shanghai 200434
China
Tel: +86 021 31260822

books@imagespublishing.com
www.imagespublishing.com

Barbara Ballinger, Margaret Crane and Images Publishing would like to profusely thank all involved photographers for their kind permission to reproduce their images, and all participating designers, architects, real estate salespeople, homeowners, and marketing experts for their valued cooperation. All known contributors are named throughout, and on pages 264–267. All photography is attributed in the Photographer Credits on page 269 unless otherwise noted.

Back cover images (clockwise from top left, see pages in brackets for original captions): Outdoor kitchen by Robert S. Hursthouse and Jeffrey A. True, Hursthouse, Inc. (see page 201), Photography by Hursthouse, Inc.; Kitchen by Tiffany Mansfield and Lisa O'Neil, Mansfield + O'Neil Interior Design, and Fergus Garber Architects (see page 189), Photography by Paul Dyer; Kitchen by Andrew Franz, AIA, Andrew Franz Architect (see page 133), Photography by Albert Vecerka/Esto, courtesy Andrew Franz Architect; Kitchen by Nicole Ellis Semple, Semple + Rappe Architects, (see page 36), Photography by Leslie Schwartz Architectural Photography; Kitchen by Nathan Kipnis, FAIA, LEED BD+C, Kipnis Architecture + Planning (see page 44), Photography by Michael Alan Kaskel; Kitchen by Richard Landry, Landry Design Group, and Merkoh Development (see page 23), Photography by Manolo Langis

A catalogue record for this book is available from the National Library of Australia

Title: Kitchen Conversations: Sharing Secrets to Kitchen Design Success // Barbara Ballinger and Margaret Crane
ISBN: 9781864709629

MIX
Paper | Supporting responsible forestry
FSC® C019910

This title was commissioned in IMAGES' Melbourne office and produced as follows:
Editorial Georgia (Gina) Tsarouhas, Danielle Hampshire *Art direction/production* Nicole Boehringer
Printed on 157gsm Chinese OJI matt art paper (FSC®) in China by Artron Art Group